As I personally experienced Jonathan deal with the loss of his amazing wife, I remember telling him how much I admired him through that most difficult time in his life. His grief was great, but the grace God gave him through it was evidently greater. Jonathan's story of real grief provides a palatable blueprint that I know all readers can glean from as they walk through life with loss. I know this personally, as I glean from his strength every day with the grief I am now experiencing.

—*Jonathan Evans*, author, speaker, chaplain of the Dallas Cowboys

Jonathan Pitts' honest, captivating, and riveting story will move your heart. His resolve and steady faith will be sure to encourage you through whatever "Wynter season" you are facing.

—*Anthony Evans*, worship leader, recording artist

This man and this message will change your life. I'm convinced of this because they've both changed mine. Jonathan Pitts built a beautiful life with my cousin and best friend, Wynter, before it was cut short by her sudden death. In these pages, he shares their story with an openness and vulnerability that will not only grip your soul but will guide you as you walk through difficulties of your own. Each page shimmers with the kind of integrity and strength that can only be shaped through brokenness, cleansed by tears, and forged by fire. This is legacy on paper.

Read it. And then pass it along to someone else. You'll be glad you did.

—*Priscilla Shirer*, Bible teacher, author

In *My Wynter Season*, Jonathan Pitts shares his very personal experience of loving Wynter, learning from Wynter, and living through the most painful and piercing time in his life as a husband wrestling with the loss of his wife. Jonathan shares an honest and detailed account of his life with Wynter and his journey through a winter season without her. His story will rivet you but, more importantly, his revelations will guide you to a place of peace, helping you to see and believe that God can use each season of your life for His glory and your good.

—*Chrystal Evans Hurst*, sister-cousin, author, speaker

Even during the darkest days of grief, Jonathan shares the peace, strength, and hope he and his family have found in the Lord. May the comfort the Lord has brought to him be yours as you are reminded of the faithful, loving God who is there in every aspect of your story.

—*Jeremy & Adrienne Camp*, singers, songwriters, worship leaders

In a story only he could tell, Jonathan Pitts takes us into the depths of a soul walking bravely through trauma with gratitude and glory. This intimate tribute to Wynter is both a call to live fearless and a caution to never assume you know God's plan. Every day matters, and *My Wynter Season* is evidence you are never alone when confronted with life's tragic turns.

—*Gabe and Rebekah Lyons*, bestselling authors, founders of Q Ideas

I read this book through tear-glazed eyes as Jonathan tells his personal story of gain, loss, grief, and hope, and the comfort and peace that Jesus brought in the midst of every season. Praise God for the hope we have in *Him*. Jonathan encourages us to keep looking toward eternity even in the darkest hours. There is a better home awaiting us in the arms of Jesus! I will never forget Wynter and the legacy she left that Jonathan and their girls are so brilliantly carrying on.

—*Candace Cameron Bure*, actress, producer, author

I met Jonathan at the funeral of his wife and my friend, Wynter. Since that day, I have watched him carry his weight of grief and sorrow with such grace, wisdom, and vulnerability. These words are ones that he has lived and ones that he is offering to us all as a balm to our own grief. Jonathan pushes us all toward Jesus and the hope that only He can provide through these words, and I do not doubt that when I walk through my next season of grief, these words will be a guide for me. You will know more about Wynter as you read this book, but most importantly, you will learn more about Jesus—the one we are all clinging to throughout our lives.

—*Jamie Ivey*, podcast host, bestselling author

MY WYNTER SEASON

JONATHAN PITTS

HARVEST HOUSE PUBLISHERS
EUGENE, OREGON

Cover by Faceout Studio

Cover photo of Wynter and Jonathan's wedding by JD Howard Photography

Cover photo © Taigi, siloto, Shebeko / Shutterstock

Interior layout by KUHN Design Group

Interior credit quote taken from *What Happens After You Die* by Randy Frazee. Copyright © 2017 by Randy Frazee. Used by permission of Thomas Nelson. www.thomasnelson.com

For bulk, special sales, or ministry purchases, please call 1-800-547-8979. Email: Customerservice@hhpbooks.com

My Wynter Season
Copyright © 2021 by Jonathan Pitts
Published by Harvest House Publishers
Eugene, Oregon 97408
www.harvesthousepublishers.com

ISBN 978-0-7369-8135-4 (pbk.)
ISBN 978-0-7369-8136-1 (eBook)

Library of Congress Control Number 2020946057

Printed in the United States of America

20 21 22 23 24 25 26 27 28 29 / VP-SK / 10 9 8 7 6 5 4 3 2 1

To the woman who was patient with me, who saw me in all of my weaknesses and imperfections and loved me selflessly anyway. I am the man I am today, in large part, because of you. You've given me incredible gifts in Alena, Kaitlyn, Camryn, and Olivia. You've entrusted me with much, and it's my joy to continue stewarding all that we built together.

Thank you, Wynter Danielle Pitts.

It was my joy to cover you, and it continues to be my joy to honor you.

I'll see you soon.

To those who have had no agony Jesus says,
"I have nothing for you;
stand on your own feet, square your own shoulders.
I have come for the man who knows he has
a bigger handful than he can cope with,
who knows there are forces he cannot touch;
I will do everything for him if he will let Me.
Only let a man grant he needs it, and I will do it for him."

OSWALD CHAMBERS,
The Shadow of an Agony

CONTENTS

FOREWORD

DR. TONY EVANS

first met Jonathan when he married my dear niece, Wynter. They were in their early twenties and starting a new life together, expecting God to do big things when they moved to Texas on a whim. We welcomed them and their daughters into our family as if they had always been around.

Little did I know the depth to the relationship we would form both as family and as co-laborers in the kingdom.

From Christmases to Fourth of July holidays to our monthly Sunday family gatherings, the richness and fullness of life only seemed to get better. Wynter and Jonathan raised their kids alongside my grandkids, all of whom affectionately call me Poppy. And as God would have it, Jonathan would spend more than 14 years working in our family's various ministries. His unique giftings worked synergistically with ours and led to incredibly productive and enjoyable years of ministry together.

Time went on, and life was good until it wasn't, and what ensued was what I refer to as "that day." The day or season when it seemed that hell broke loose.

It started with the slow and painful loss of my younger brother. That pain was excruciating, but what came next was one of the most sudden and shocking losses I'd ever experienced. Wynter, my baby brother's daughter and Jonathan's wife, left this world. Without notice she was gone, and our family was overcome with shock and sadness.

I was there when Jonathan told his girls their mother was gone. I officiated Wynter's funeral. And watching Jonathan lead his family through that time had a significant impact on me personally. It was as if God was using him to show me what it would look like to walk through similar pain. He spoke with a conviction and a resolve that can only come from a man leaning into a faith stored deep within.

Little did I know how much I'd need that insight because our pain would grow as our family losses continued to mount.

My sister and her husband were next, joining the others in eternity, both within a year of Wynter's passing.

Nothing could prepare me for the next season that raised its ugly head most personally for me. Less than a year and a half after losing Wynter, I lost my hero and father, Arthur. And as if the pain couldn't get any worse, the next month I faced the most difficult day of my life when my wife of 50 years, Lois, succumbed to an intense battle with cancer, joining the parade of family members into the presence of Jesus. On that day, I was the man leaning into a faith stored deep within and supported and held by loved ones surrounding me.

This season has marked our family. This season has marked me. And this season has marked Jonathan.

What you will find in this book is a faith that, if you lean into it with an open mind and heart, will mark *your* life with a trust that only God can give when "that day" comes for you. Maybe that day is now. If not, I assure you that day is coming. Lean in.

1

A MORNING'S RUN, 2018

My alarm, with a persistent urgency, woke me from a deep sleep at 5:30 a.m. I was still tired and sleeping in an unfamiliar bed, but I knew I should keep up my normal morning routine and take a run to get the day started. Over the years, I've learned that running will do me much more good than simply rolling over and getting a little more sleep. So, I climbed out of bed and felt my feet come to rest on the cold hardwood floor. That sensation jolted me awake, and I pressed the button on my phone to keep it quiet, so I wouldn't wake my wife, Wynter, who continued to sleep soundly. She was not a morning person. If I woke her early in the morning, she'd let me know in no uncertain terms that she was not very happy about it. After just over 15 years of marriage, I had managed to learn that lesson. When you love someone, you honor their desires, such as hers to sleep soundly through the early morning hours.

I closed the door to the bathroom and flipped on the light, then scrolled through the notifications that had come in on my phone during the last seven hours. Most of them didn't seem important, but one of them caught my attention. It read: "Do you have an exit strategy?" Not wanting to take the time right then, I made a mental note to check it out later. I had an interest in helping ministries transition leaders well, and I assumed the article had to do with leadership transitions. Little did I know how much this question would haunt and inform the days that followed.

In almost every way, it seemed like a normal Tuesday morning.

As I pulled on my running clothes, I looked for some music to accompany me on my run—just the motivation I needed to get me out the door. It was still dark, and the route wouldn't be familiar. Our family was staying in the home of Wynter's cousin while we awaited the last pieces to come into place for our move from Dallas, Texas, to Franklin, Tennessee.

Wynter's first cousin Priscilla Shirer is a well-known Bible teacher and conference leader. One of many in the Evans' clan to commit themselves to public ministry. Priscilla had been kind enough to let us crash at her house while we made the final preparations for our big move. This kindness is typical for Priscilla, who we just call "Silla." To our kids, she is "Auntie Silla."

The Evans family had become as close to us as though they were immediate family. Priscilla is like a sister to me, Dr. Evans and his late wife, Lois, are like a spiritual mom and dad, and their three other kiddos—Chrystal, Anthony, and Jonathan—are like siblings as well. Our kids had grown up with theirs and leaving them behind would be the most difficult part of our journey.

Our house had already sold, so it was great to have a comfortable place to finalize all the preparations for the move and prepare our hearts for the transition. It would be a big change in our lives. We'd lived in Dallas for most of our married life, and I had worked as an executive for Dr. Tony Evans's ministry, The Urban Alternative. Dr. Evans was my boss, and Wynter was the daughter of his baby brother. I'd loved my time with the ministry, enjoyed rising to all the new challenges, and believed I'd had a significant impact, but now sensed it was time to move on when I was offered a pastoral position in a large family of churches in Tennessee called Church of the City. I felt called to be a part of what was happening there, and God had made it clear that my family's story was supposed to merge with theirs.

I closed the back door as quietly as I could in order not to wake my family and let my eyes adjust for a minute to the pitch blackness outside. Then, knowing that I needed to pay careful attention to where I was going, I started down the winding road of the country neighborhood in which our guest home was located. Even in the daytime, we had to be careful about driving these twisting roads, with their deep ditches that flanked each side of the narrow road, made even more hazardous by the trees, mailboxes, and four-board fences that crept into the space where I was now running. So, jogging along while it was still dark made it even more important to be extra careful.

That morning any anxiety about the big changes ahead was dwarfed by a feeling of peace and contentment. Our 14 years in Texas, which accounted for nearly all our years together, had been good ones. With three of our four girls being born in Dallas, slowly but surely, we'd become Texans. Even in our leaving we all sensed that wouldn't change. The great state of Texas was a part of us, and its expansive borders opened our imaginations wider for what lay ahead.

It was hard to say goodbye, but we knew our close connection with family would always be there, even across however many miles separated us. Two days earlier, we had celebrated a birthday with the extended family, and it was a magical afternoon, though it contained a twinge of sadness about the coming separation.

I thought about what the next month would hold in store. First there would be the tearful goodbyes, and then the long drive to Franklin, Tennessee, just outside Nashville. We'd already made a preliminary trip to Franklin so that we could close on our new home just the week before. After unpacking all our stuff, we'd had four days before we made an equally long trip to Iowa for a family reunion on my mother's side, as well as a celebration of my grandmother's ninety-fourth birthday. This turned out to be an amazing family vacation, and all of us had fun engaging with all my siblings and my 13 nieces and nephews. But when it was over, we found ourselves weary and tired as we returned to Texas for my final week of wrapping things up at The Urban Alternative.

I ran more slowly than usual, making sure to feel the pavement under my feet since I couldn't really see very well. Honestly, I really couldn't see a thing! I kept an eye out for cars that might be traveling this road early in the morning and not expecting to come across a jogger. I was listening to worship music through my earbuds and singing along under my breath. My heart was filled with gratitude for God's goodness to me and my family. The warm, damp Texas morning was so familiar to me that it felt like a blanket of love as I did a little talking with God about the future.

As I whispered a prayer to the Lord, I felt Him whisper back, and I had a sudden urge to pray for my girls, name by name. It was a nudging from God that I couldn't ignore, so I lifted each of them up to God, asking Him for His protection and presence in each of their lives. I was confident God would be with our family as we began this next chapter of our story, and I felt an amazing confidence about heading into the adventure that lay ahead. I imagined great days to come. I was expectant.

I arrived back at the house, satisfied and energized. Wynter was still asleep. On my way to the shower, I said a little prayer for her, pausing to watch her breath rise and fall. My heart was full of love for her and gratitude that God had put the two of us together. We had come a long way, and we were in unison about how that journey would continue. I knew how blessed I was to have such a confident and inspiring woman as my closest friend. As I dressed, a peace descended upon my heart. Driving to the office, I thought about the loose ends I still needed to take care of before we set out on our new life in Tennessee.

Pulling into my parking spot at The Urban Alternative, I thought about the people I worked with and how they were like a family to me. I was responsible for overseeing a little over 30 people, each of whom had a special place in my heart. It had been such a privilege to work closely with Dr. Evans and his wife, Lois. His teaching and the ministry's distribution of it through radio and television broadcasts, print, digital, and various other forms, accomplished so much for the Kingdom of

God and changed so many lives—mine included. I couldn't have been more grateful to serve such a ministry and such a man.

It had been a challenge at first. I'd had to step up and take a lot of responsibility. Frankly, it was a job that I had to grow into, but the Evanses were always patient with me and always encouraging. I always joked that as a grafted-in family member by marriage, I was "close enough to be trusted, but far enough away to be fired"! It was a line that could always lighten a room. But in all seriousness, their trust in me, example to me, and the work I did with them and for them, had changed me forever.

It was an emotional last week, and a reminder of the grace God had given me in letting me work with this amazing group of people. There was so much to do on my final day that it just flew by, but just before leaving I had one more important task to accomplish. I needed to sign off on a book manuscript.

Wynter and I had written a book on marriage called *Emptied*. I think both of us felt like we were in over our heads giving other people advice about their marriages, but we also knew that God had taught us a way of working together that had made all the difference in our relationship. So, when our publisher had asked us to consider telling our story about marriage, we said yes. But, we warned, it would not be a "how-to" book from experts, but an invitation to join us on the journey, a warts-and-all look at how we'd learned to build a strong connection with each other and how we'd learned to make Jesus central to our marriage. We'd had a great time writing it, even as it brought new issues to the surface that we had to work on! When it was finished and we sent it off to the publisher, we felt really proud of what we had written and were convinced that it could help other people find the kind of joy in their marriage that we had found in ours.

Now, as I held the edited version in my hands, I was happy we had said yes. Along with the manuscript was a consent form we needed to sign, agreeing to the edits and locking down the final version. We needed to get this returned to the publisher before we set out on our move, so I signed at the bottom, and, with Wynter's permission, signed her name as well. (Shh…don't tell our publisher!) I didn't know it at that moment, but as I attached the document to an email and sent it off, I was sealing a time capsule. This book would be, in a sense, the summation of our lives together.

Exactly three hours later, Wynter passed from this world into the arms of Jesus.

⟞⟨⟩⟞

This book is my story of losing the most wonderful gift I'd ever been given and of the struggle to make sense of life without her. Let me tell you, it has been a difficult journey. But in the middle of that journey of grief, I have learned so much about myself, my friends, and my family, and I want to share a little of that with you. I'm not sure how I could have traveled this dark road without being surrounded by their love and care. Even more, I have felt surrounded by the love of God, and I have learned that some of the truths about Him that were only abstract ideas before have now become truths that I know from experience. He has been with me every single step of the way. He has surrounded me with love.

2

THE MEETING, 2001

I think I loved her from the moment I first saw her. We both had been making our way through our lives, just minding our own business, and then God stepped in.

I was in the middle of a five-year program at Drexel University in Philadelphia, and not really thinking that much about being in a serious relationship. I was too busy and too focused on school. But I was also, deep down, a little bit lonely.

I was leaving my dorm one cold morning, making my way to class, when I stepped out onto the normally crowded sidewalks of Philly. For some reason, the streets were quiet that morning, which allowed me to catch a glimpse of a strikingly beautiful young woman. She caught my attention immediately. Maybe it was partially something about the confidence in her step. She always moved like a woman on a mission. Or maybe it was her beauty. Whatever it was, I was struck with a desire to get to know her someday. After that first sighting, I kept noticing her pretty regularly on my daily walks to class.

In time, I learned that we were both part of the same freshman class, but with opposite co-op education programs and internships abroad, we hadn't ever come into contact with each other. Then, just days after September 11, 2001 (and about a year after seeing her for the first time), we ran into each other at a party. I got up the courage to talk with her, and we ended up in a long and incredibly enjoyable conversation. She was clearly not only beautiful, but smart—very smart. We chatted away, and then I took the risk of asking for her phone number. She scribbled it down and, with a smile, I tucked it into my pocket.

And then I got nervous. I had her number, but I didn't have much self-confidence and couldn't bring myself to dial her number. I was afraid of being rejected, I guess. So I put it off.

A few weeks later, this normally rather quiet young lady saw me across the courtyard and tracked me down. "Why haven't you called me yet?" she wanted to know.

My response was quick and off the cuff, "I don't know."

I gave it 24 hours for good measure, and then I called and invited her on a date. She said yes.

Ever the romantic that I am, our first date was the film *Monsters, Inc.* And in the next few days and conversation that followed, I became absolutely convinced that she was the one. I knew that my life would be changed forever because I had met her.

She came out of nowhere. Wynter entered my life like a season unannounced, and she was there to stay.

I'd been looking to temporary relationships, beer, and my buddies to keep my loneliness at bay, but nothing really worked. Not until I met her. We went deep very quickly in conversation and discovered a commonality in our faith, and our love grew deep just as quickly. We felt as if we were made for each other.

Within seven months, we were engaged, both of us grateful and surprised about what God had done in bringing us together. We'd both grown up in Christian homes, and we both had a love for Jesus, but there was something about finding each other that drew us even closer to Him. Our meeting was like an intervention from heaven. We began to challenge each other in ways that would help us shed those parts of ourselves that didn't match up to the identity we knew was ours in Christ.

We married on June 27, 2003, just two weeks after we both graduated. We each had our goals. She wanted to be a barista in Italy, and I, who had spent several years in the Army Reserve Officers Training Corps, was scheduled to be commissioned into the army upon graduation. It ended up that I received a medical discharge, so I didn't deploy to Iraq with many of the guys I had trained with. And she was willing to forgo her dream of coffee, wine, and Italian culture to make a commitment to me.

We settled in New Jersey, where I had grown up, and had our first child, Alena. When we moved to Texas shortly thereafter, both sets of parents weren't too happy about having their grandchild move more than 1,300 miles away. In Texas, three more daughters were born: Kaitlyn and the twins, Camryn and Olivia. At first, I worked with Wynter's cousin Anthony, an incredible vocalist and worship leader, who was launching his career fresh off his time as a singer with gospel icon Kirk Franklin. He toured and traveled around the country giving concerts during the week and leading worship on the weekends. Our friendship began as I helped him out by selling CDs and other merchandise wherever he went. From those simple beginnings grew a ministry of multiple albums and a career for him and a job as his manager for me. Along the way, we developed a brotherly friendship that has lasted to this day. My time with him ended just after he made a splash as a finalist on NBC's television program *The Voice*. Eventually, this would open the door to working with his father, Dr. Tony Evans, in his nonprofit ministry, The Urban Alternative.

Wynter was trained as a grant writer, which is what initially brought us to Texas, but she soon tired of working in the business side of ministry and decided to focus her efforts on raising our girls. She sensed that it was God's will. That change proved to be a challenge for her at first, because she felt she kind of lost herself in the job of being a mother. As much as she loved being with her girls full-time, she missed the traveling and status of being on a career track. In the struggle to adapt, she leaned heavily on the words of Psalm 37:4: "Delight yourself in the LORD; and He will give you the desires of your heart" (NASB). One of her greatest desires was to write, and eventually she found a way to use that gift.

I never noticed a ton of drive in Wynter. Anyone who knew her would tell you that she was about as relaxed as anyone you could find. She was mostly content to "go with the flow." That was, until she found her passion. She had a deep conviction and drive for helping our daughters know and love Jesus in a real way. Over many years of growth, she discovered that God loved her for her, not for some future version of her, and she wanted with all her heart to help our girls know the same. But she didn't want them to have to wait to discover that.

That passion led to the creation of a small, homemade resource that was originally just intended for our girls. She downloaded a free copy of Adobe InDesign and taught herself how to use it to create something that was spiritually inspiring, practical, and fun. Something that would entertain and stir their natural creativity, while at the same time helping them learn some lessons that would guide them in their walk with God. She called it *For Girls Like You*, and the magazine was intentionally targeted to young girls who wanted something they could call their own. At first this seemed like an expensive hobby, but Wynter's skills in design and writing continued to develop.

She was surprised by how much fun she had putting it together, and how much our daughters loved it. Soon friends were wanting copies for their families, and then they told their friends, and soon she had a growing following of young moms with the same conviction. God had taken something small and made it into something of growing significance for scores of young girls. The demand grew, and Wynter continued to excel in the creation of the magazine. What once looked handmade, now had a professional gloss. What was once just a little something to keep the girls interested had become a full-grown ministry. There was no plan. There was no strategy. There was just a diligent woman with an incredible voice for girls "just like her."

That's the way God works. He enters into each of our stories, takes our small talents, and creates something special from them. He takes the ordinary and makes it extraordinary. The sense of purpose that Wynter had previously found in her business career was nothing compared to the sense of purpose He gave her in her new ministry to girls.

And as time went on, I even found myself becoming more involved, as it became too much for Wynter to handle on her own.

—⊸⊱⊰⊶—

I can see now that the lessons of Wynter's life are relevant for all of us. God had an amazing purpose and plan for her life, and it still carries that meaning and value. He has the same for you. One of the reasons I wrote this book was to help you to see that. He has gifts He has given you that He wants you to use—talents. And He has gifts that He wants to give you that He wants you to lean into—relationships. I'm so proud of Wynter for seeing this before it was too late and maximizing both her talents and her relationships. The world is a better place because she saw this.

I'm a better man because of Wynter.

My girls are stronger women because of Wynter.

And thousands of girls are becoming more like Christ because of Wynter.

Through all the challenges we confronted as a couple, we had the support of each other helping us to face them. Then, when God took her home, I realized two things. First, that I would always miss her and the unique joy that she brought to my life, and second, that God wouldn't abandon me in the dark hours after her death—that He was always there, always with me.

3

TRAVELING

Other than me and the girls, Wynter's favorite things were travel…
and napping. And if she could nap while traveling, that was the
ultimate bliss for her! It's a good thing that she loved traveling, because
she did a lot of it during her life.

Born in west Baltimore, she was raised in a densely populated area
notorious for drugs, gang violence, and poverty. It's no wonder that
she was glad to escape the city as soon as she could. Thanks to the fervent prayers of her mother and grandmother, she was accepted into one
of the top all-girl private schools in Maryland. They didn't have any-
where near the needed money for tuition at such a prestigious place,
but God opened doors for financial aid and scholarships. Still, there
was a requirement that her family kick in some money for the tuition,
so they had to constantly trust God to bring in a little extra that could
be invested in Wynter's education. And God never let them down.

Money for school wasn't the only challenge. They also had to figure
out how to get her to classes, which were on the other side of the city.
Since her mother and grandmother both worked, she had to depend
upon public transportation. This meant that every day she had to pass
the drug dealers who hung out on the corner a few blocks away from
the bus stop. Even years later, when visiting her family home, Wynter
and I could watch drug deals going down on that same corner. As a

young child, she saw people shooting up in their parked cars and witnessed fights over drug money. Wynter would have to switch buses several times on the long route to the school, carried away from the blocks of inner-city row houses and through neighborhoods made up of single family dwellings, and then eventually to the school, which was in one of the nicest areas of the city. When she stepped off the bus, she was in a different world—one of wealth and privilege and opportunity. It was a world where she felt like she didn't fit at first, but soon she found her way.

At first, she was often afraid. But she never spoke of her fear or her nervousness to her family. They had invested so much. Besides, Wynter's grandmother was a woman of prayer, and her granddaughter's safety was one of the prime targets of those prayers.

This experience left an indelible mark on Wynter's life, as though God was using it to condition her heart for a willingness to go. She had the street girl savvy that came from her inner-city upbringing, and an intelligence that was molded by a great education. And she had grit. As she grew, and life brought new challenges, she became unafraid to face anything that came her way. And she always carried herself with elegance and grace.

So, when she got the chance to travel to France as an exchange student during high school, she jumped at the opportunity. Her adventures abroad taught her to love Europe, which was something she felt until the end of her life. After graduation, she traveled a hundred miles up I-95 from Baltimore to Philadelphia, where she attended college. There she took advantage of a program to study abroad and spent a semester in London, from where she visited places all over Europe. Her favorite was Italy. I eventually became the primary thing standing in the way of her dream of being a barista somewhere in Rome or Florence. She loved the Italian pace of life, so much more laid back than the "go until you drop" ethos of the United States. Two of the things she taught me were how to dial it back a little, and how to appreciate the luxury of a midday nap.

One of the highlights of our years together was celebrating our fourteenth anniversary in Maui. Because my work with Dr. Evans involved flying around to meet with donors, I had accumulated a lot of flyer miles and hotel points, so we decided to go to Hawaii in style. Our flights were covered by points, and we stayed at the Ritz Carlton in Kapalua for eight nights. It was as top notch as top notch gets. We didn't just have a room. We had a suite. It was amazing, and from then on Wynter wanted this kind of luxury to be our new normal. She loved to aim high! Though she was a practical person, she never minded being pampered!

Over the years, we visited Alaska, various Hawaiian Islands, Mexico, the Caribbean, and all over the United States. Much of our travel was related to the ministry we were doing. She even went to Uganda to write the story of a ministry that was saving the lives of children. She spoke at a bunch of different conferences, and she got to visit the Holy Land, Israel, about two years before her death. I'm so glad she got to see Jerusalem before she went to dwell in the New Jerusalem. As much as she always loved Italy, after that trip Israel became her new favorite place—a place where the world of the Bible came alive before her eyes. It deepened her confidence in God and His miraculous goodness to His people.

⸺⸺

Seasons come and seasons go, but Wynter surely left too soon. Our years as a couple blur together sometimes. It is hard to remember all that we experienced together; though, other than my family of origin, there is no one to whom I've been committed for as long as I was to her.

Somehow her name always makes me think of the snowy Rocky Mountains in winter—beautiful, serene, and reaching heavenward. She was a complex woman—a mixture of simplicity and elegance, truly classy in every way. But she never put on airs, and she made everyone she met feel important and loved. Our relationship matured like a fine wine, growing more wonderful with every passing year. Each day I spent with her left me wanting more days to be together. Wynter was my home, like a cabin in the forest with a warm wood fireplace. She was always there to warm me when I came in from the elements—both metaphorically and literally.

I'm a fairly high-strung guy, and I needed Wynter's calm demeanor to settle me down sometimes. She could make me feel a peace and tranquility that wasn't normal for me. She had a slow, steady rhythm with which she approached life, and her serenity helped me find a better way of approaching each day. I don't want to leave the impression that everything was always perfect. Like every couple, we had our disagreements and squabbles, but I never doubted how much she loved me, and I made sure she knew the depth of my love for her. Our love was not just an infatuation. It was built upon the deepest sort of friendship. There was no one I enjoyed being with more than her.

Wynter was my girl, though she always hated it when I referred to her as that. She'd snap back, "I am not a girl! I am a woman!" Truth is, she was both. She had a sweet, childlike innocence, as well as a strong and bold confidence. I respected her just as much as I loved her.

It may sound like a cliché, but I truly believe that ours was a marriage made in heaven.

That's why it felt so devastating when I lost her.

4

FINAL HOURS

After leaving the office that day, I picked up our van, which I'd left to be cleaned and detailed. It sparkled like new as I drove to Costco to pick up some items we'd need for our long journey.

My phone buzzed, letting me know I'd received a text message. It was from Wynter, and it was very brief: "I feel…" with a green, sour-faced emoji tacked on to represent "sick."

"What's wrong?" I texted back.

I got no response, but then again it wasn't that unusual for Wynter to struggle with a bout of nausea. It also wasn't unusual for her to be nonresponsive to my text messages.

I stopped at Costco and bought the fixings for a simple but tasty meal of pork ribs and salad, thinking that I could take care of dinner and she wouldn't have to worry about cooking. Earlier in the day, she'd used a "walkie-talkie" app to leave me a message: "Please be on tonight." I knew what she meant by that. She was graciously requesting my full attention and energy because she had another book deadline bearing down on her (beyond the one I'd just signed and sent off). She was running two weeks late and knew the next couple weeks, with moving and all, would not be an easy time to try to finish it. She was asking for freedom to disappear mentally in order to tap into her creative juices. Plus, she would need some silence and some mental quiet, which were often in short supply in our busy home. My job, then, was to keep the girls busy so that Wynter could complete her book.

This young and carefree girl I'd married had become a publishing machine. Over the last seven years, she had continued to pour her heart and soul into the *For Girls Like You* magazine, which had grown by leaps and bounds, while at the same time publishing no fewer than seven books! Our now-finalized book on marriage was number eight, and she was trying to complete number nine, titled *I Am Yours: Prayers for God's Girls*. Priscilla Shirer would later call this last book, full of short devotions and bold, heartfelt prayers, "Wynter's Last Will and Testament." Because of her heart for girls, it seems appropriate that this would be the inheritance she was leaving behind for all her young readers. But most of all, these prayers are a lasting gift to the four daughters she loved so much.

Passing through the front gate, I was surprised to see my sister-in-law's van in the driveway. Andrea had married Wynter's brother five years before our wedding, and the two sisters-in-law had grown into very close friends. Andrea and her husband also served as mentors and living examples of what a strong marriage looks like. They rarely offered advice, but their lives spoke volumes. They were not just family. They were our best friends.

As I entered through the back door, I could hear the sound of laughter echoing through the house. I found everyone sitting in the living room on the L-shaped sectional couch as they worked on each other's hair and played some sort of word game. "You can be a dog, but you can't be a hippo," someone said. "You can be an elephant, but you can't be a cat," was the answer. I had to smile at the silliness. I'd worried, based on her earlier text, that the atmosphere at home might be a little heavy, but the gentle smile and frequent outbursts of laughter from Wynter assured me that all was just fine.

I whispered in her ear that I was going to take a quick power nap, and she nodded approvingly. I knew this would give me the energy I needed to be "on." I roused myself about 20 minutes later, hearing Andrea and her kids leaving. It was time for me to make some space for Wynter, so I unpackaged the dinner and got started. She told me she was needing a bit of rest. I asked her if she was going to want some food, but she just shrugged, meaning she wasn't sure, and wandered into the bedroom to lie down. Nothing unusual here. She nearly always took a late afternoon nap.

Shortly after that, I finished the meal and began to fill the girls' plates, so I gently opened the bedroom door to ask Wynter, "You think you want to eat dinner, babe?"

"I think I'm going to lay here just a bit longer," she replied.

As we finished dinner, I felt a few annoying strands of pulled pork left wedged between my teeth, which is something I really hate. So, I walked past the living room, quietly entered the bedroom, and walked past her quiet, petite frame to the master bathroom, where I was able to floss the offending pieces of meat out of my teeth. I paced quietly in the bedroom as I flossed. I hate standing still to floss. Flossing is boring enough as it is, so movement always helped me get through the task.

Then I noticed that something was wrong. Wynter had been sleeping when I entered, her tiny body almost lost in the big, king-size bed. Now she was sitting up, her back facing away from me. Suddenly, she slumped over into an odd and uncomfortable position. I wondered for a moment if she just had decided to get a little more rest, but then I heard her quietly moaning.

I rushed to the bed and turned her over to face me. That's when I knew something was very wrong. Her eyes were open, but lifeless.

A feeling of incredible concern swept over me, and all my senses heightened in a nanosecond. I patted her face to try to rouse her, thinking that maybe she was just having a hard time coming out of sleep.

"Babe," I whispered desperately.

Her only response was a heartrending moan.

"Wynter...Wynter...stay with me," I said more loudly, patting her face a bit more firmly.

No response.

I ran over the possibilities in my mind. *Is she just sleeping more soundly than usual? Was this some sort of seizure?*

I knew things were serious when I decided to sweep her throat to see if she was choking and found that it was clear.

I quickly lifted her unmoving body from the bed and laid her gently on the floor to try CPR. I still remember the weight as her limbs hung lifeless. I'd been an Eagle Scout, so I'd been trained in CPR. As I rested her on the floor, I still remember the coolness and hardness of the ribbed wood beneath my feet. I started in with chest compressions and mouth-to-mouth resuscitation while I yelled for the girls to bring me my phone. My efforts weren't seeming to have much effect.

This was the single most horrifying moment of my entire life. The girls didn't know at first if this was some sort of bad joke, but they quickly realized what was going on. I called 911. I called Priscilla and Andrea to ask them to pray. It was all so surreal.

I asked the girls to go outside and wait for one of their aunties to show up.

It took over 12 minutes for the ambulance to arrive, which seemed like an eternity. I kept attempting CPR, but it wasn't making a difference. It is one thing to perform it on a practice dummy, but it was quite another to perform it on my beautiful, fragile wife. I didn't want to injure her or make things worse. I kept praying aloud, but never stopped working.

There was no discernible heartbeat. I knew this because I knew the distinctly slushy and heavy sound her heart normally made, the result of a heart murmur with which she'd been diagnosed as a child. She'd had mitral valve prolapse her whole life. In layman's terms, a leaky heart valve. The door to her valve flapped as blood gushed through instead of opening and closing cleanly. She also had a blood-clotting disorder that we discovered during her first pregnancy. But as long as she saw a cardiologist once a year, there hadn't been any trouble other than a scare while pregnant with our firstborn, Alena. In that case, there had been what can only be described as a miracle.

That was what we needed now. A miracle. I prayed for one, trying to stay calm for the sake of my girls. I was all adrenaline. No flight. All fight. Fighting as best as I could for her life.

When the paramedics arrived, they radiated calm and composure, and when I started asking too many questions, they suggested I wait outside. I sent thoughts toward Wynter, pleading, "Don't leave me.

Stay with me." I think, in that moment, I knew I was losing her and that she was leaving for another place, and so I didn't pray "Don't let her die," but "Don't let her leave." I didn't want the Lord to take her from me.

Back when I first started working for Dr. Evans, I was very afraid of flying. It was a fear that had built up over my years as a dad. With each new daughter, my fear just increased a little bit more. When my twins (daughters number three and four) arrived, that fear hit an all-time high. And I flew way too much to be experiencing any sort of flight phobia.

At any bit of turbulence, I would nervously grip the armrests for dear life, playing out a horrible scenario in my mind where the plane would drop out of the sky. I couldn't sleep or get much work done on the flights because I was so overwhelmed by fear. In my desperation, God led me to a scripture which I memorized and recited to myself every time I took a trip on an airplane: "Have no fear of sudden disaster or of the ruin that overtakes the wicked, for the LORD will be at your side and will keep your foot from being snared" (Proverbs 3:25-26).

God gave me this verse to overcome my fear of flying, but that trial was a test for the moment I now found myself in. I had internalized it and come to trust in its message. But now it became even more real to me. I realized it wasn't so much a promise that nothing bad would ever happen to someone who loves God, but a promise that God would be there beside you at all times—no matter what.

In the present context, this spoke to me so powerfully. Even as the light went out in Wynter's eyes, I knew God was with her. He was at her side, walking next to her at every step. And this meant that I could trust that Wynter was safe. She was okay. It meant that even though I couldn't protect her right now, that didn't mean she wasn't being protected. And God was also with me, in all my confusion and worry and fear. I didn't have to face it alone.

As the paramedics wheeled her out the front door, I prayed for a miracle. It had been at least 20 minutes since she had first started exhibiting symptoms. In some ways, though, it seemed like hours had passed, and there wasn't much indication that her body was responding to any of the attempts made to revive her. The paramedics loaded her into the ambulance, and as it pulled away, I jumped in the car with the neighbors from across the street, who followed the ambulance to the hospital. Drea, my daughters' aunt, was on her way to pick up the girls and meet us there. We were mostly quiet on the ride, and in my mind I was processing the odds of recovery given the length of time that had elapsed and how far gone she seemed. Between racing thoughts, I prayed. A simple, desperate prayer: "God, don't let her leave. Don't take her." It was all I could muster. I busily sent text messages and prayer requests as the miles ticked by:

"Wynter is not breathing and we are on our way to the hospital. Please pray."

———

I soon found myself pacing up and down in the hallway outside of the emergency room. I wasn't allowed into the room while they worked on saving Wynter's life. I stopped for a moment and gazed at the light coming from inside the room through a little window above the door. I could hear the bustling movement coming from the staff who were trying to revive her lifeless body, and the random beeps of the equipment they were using. One of the younger doctors, who occasionally stepped out of the room to brief me on what was going on behind the closed door, was unfailingly kind and empathetic. He understood that I needed to be kept informed, and he did it in such a gentle and caring way.

Deep down, I am a manager at heart, so a thousand details were swirling around my head. I couldn't keep still, so I kept pacing. All the what-ifs and worst-case scenarios came flooding into my brain. Doing the math in my head, I understood that the length of time she'd not been breathing would make her survival unlikely. Still, I hoped and prayed, and I asked God for a miracle. "Holy Spirit," I prayed, "breathe life into her lungs." I believed that God could save her, but I also found myself saying, "I believe, Lord. Help my unbelief."

Wynter had done a lot of traveling—Israel, Uganda, and countless conferences for women and moms across the country. She had always come back. This time she was on a journey into seemingly utter darkness, and I had no certainty about her return.

I was full of all kinds of mixed emotions. My mind was having an internal argument with my soul. While my mind was telling me "you should be freaking out right now," there was a strange inner peace that was allowing me to stay calm. And even as I felt that supernatural calm, I felt a little guilty for not being "worried enough." At another level, I knew that I was putting this all into God's hands and trusting in His faithfulness.

The door to the examination room opened and one of the attending physicians came out into the hallway. His words, offered quietly and gently, were the words I didn't want to hear: "We had a pulse for a while, but it's gone. You might want to come say goodbye."

Though I had mentally prepared myself for the worst, I really had no idea how I would actually respond. And what I felt at that moment was almost like my mind and body had been taken over by God. I sensed His peace and comfort in a way I can't really even begin to explain. He was with me now.

Wynter was lying on the emergency room table. Lifeless. The mechanical chest compression unit that had been helping with resuscitation was still attached to her, and still making its methodical compressions, but it hadn't been able to help her back from the brink. There was nothing further that this group of skilled physicians could do. There was nothing I could do to help her. Her life was now in God's hands.

He was welcoming her home.

As I approached the table on which she lay, everything else around me fell away. The staff, the equipment, and the buzzing lights became a blur as my focus went straight to my beautiful girl.

I thought about how much I loved looking at her face, and the way her hair would fall on the pillow. In fact, at this moment she looked like she was taking a nap and had forgotten to wrap her hair, as she usually did to keep it from tangling. Her beautiful freckles were vivid on her small face. I gently pressed my lips and cheek against her forehead. Time seemed to stop, and everything around me just went quiet. For a moment, it was just Wynter and me. It felt as though she had left her earthly body, but she still seemed close somehow, as though she could hear me. Through much heartache and trembling, I whispered these words in her ear as I caressed her hair: "It's okay, babe. I love you, and it's okay. I will take care of the girls. You don't have to worry about them. I love you with all that I am, and you are the best thing that ever happened to me."

I shared a moment of tenderest intimacy with my Wynter, wishing that I could find better words to express all that was in my heart. I thought of so many times in the past when our tears would mingle, and we would comfort one another. I thought of how I would sometimes sing to her during the most difficult moments—when she was giving birth, when we were trying to come together after a little squabble about something inconsequential, or when she just needed some reassurance. I was never fully confident in my singing voice, but with Wynter I had full confidence. In fact, I had sung to her at our wedding. This moment was just as sacred.

So, I sang to her.

I ignored my feelings of awkwardness, surrounded by the steady thrum of the machines and the doctors looking on. I determined to spend one last moment with her in the way she always loved. It was my best way to say goodbye. I instinctively thought of a song from the group All Sons and Daughters, which perfectly expressed what I was feeling in that moment.

The song, "Great Are You, Lord," expresses the reality that it is God who puts breath into our lungs. He gives it. We use it and eventually we give it right back to Him. It's also the very thing we use to praise Him and acknowledge His greatness, in good and difficult times. This was the cry of my heart even in the face of the hardest thing I'd ever been through.

I'll never forget what I felt as I sang these words to Wynter, who I somehow knew could hear them. It was an otherworldly moment, a time when here and forever seemed to come together as I thanked God in gratitude for all we had, and love for the God who now held her in His hands. Even as I sang, I knew she was now fully experiencing the true reality of what I was singing in her ear. In that moment, so was I. I doubt I'll ever get a clearer glimpse of the love that lies beyond than I did right then and there. My fear lifted. I felt no terror. There was, instead, the deepest sort of peace which filled my soul. I could accept the sorrow because I trusted that He was faithful. I fully understood for the first time why the apostle Paul had told the Ephesians to keep on "speaking to one another with psalms, hymns, and songs from the Spirit. Sing and make music from your heart to the Lord" (Ephesians 5:19).

Months later, when I told a friend about my experience, he reminded me of these words from C.S. Lewis: "Holy places are dark places. It is life and strength, not knowledge and words, that we get in them. Holy wisdom is not clear and thin like water, but thick and dark like blood."[1]

In this "thick" moment I knew that I was not done with Wynter. I knew that one season had now passed, but that our relationship was eternal. It had just entered a new phase.

5

A SEASON OF LOSS

Wynter's passing came during a season of loss for our extended family. During the previous year, we had experienced the death of several family members. First was Wynter's uncle, Bo. She had to make an unplanned flight to Boca Raton, Florida, to say goodbye to him when his long battle with bone cancer took a turn for the worst. Because she had grown up without a father, Bo was an extremely important person in Wynter's life. In many ways, he had helped fill that hole in her life. In ways both big and small, he leveraged his life to care for Wynter and her brother, Sean. The whole family had gathered to see him one last time, and a few weeks later he would pass, leaving behind his beloved wife, whom we affectionately called "Aunt Poochie."

Wynter's passing would come just six short months later, much more unexpectedly.

Six months after Wynter's passing, Aunt Beverly, Bo's sister, unexpectedly passed away from a complication with her lungs. Like Bo, she was only in her sixties. She had also played a significant role in Wynter's upbringing in Baltimore. Shortly thereafter, Beverly's husband, who seemingly did not want to go on living without her, died rather suddenly as well.

Not long after Wynter went to be with Jesus, her grandfather started to decline. "Two Daddy," as we called him, was the patriarch of the family, and had just watched his son, Bo; his daughter, Beverly; her husband, James; and his granddaughter, Wynter, all pass within a little over a year's time. He was a man admired by everyone who knew him. He was strong, yet tender. And even as we walked this road of loss, he was first to point us to the reality of God's faithfulness. Sixteen months after Wynter died, he breathed his last breath. He had lived a long and fruitful life, so in a way, his death at age 90 seemed a bit redemptive to me. It wasn't shortened, but seemingly extended, considering the years he'd spent on the dangerous streets of Baltimore. He outlived the life expectancy for a black man in that city by many years.

All of us thought and hoped that maybe our run of deaths would be over. It was not to be. Tony's wife of 50 years, and Wynter's beloved aunt, had been diagnosed with a rare and aggressive form of cancer months prior. Tony had already lost his brother, Bo; his sister, Beverly; his brother-in-law, James; and his niece, Wynter; and now he was preparing to lose his best friend. People all over the world prayed for her, and she battled hard against the disease, but her battle came to an end just slightly less than two years after Bo's death.

I owed a lot to Aunt Lois. When she decided to retire from her role as the executive director of Dr. Evans's ministry, she personally chose me to step into her previous role. I'm sure it was quite a sacrifice for her to step aside for a young man in his early thirties who would likely lead the ministry in a much different way than she had. But that is the kind of person she was. She knew that life was lived in seasons, and so she opened up a door to a new season for me, while she stepped into a different one herself. Lois and Dr. Evans were, for our girls, just like grandparents, and they treated Wynter and me like adopted children of their own. Her passing reopened the wounds of my grief in a way that I wasn't prepared for. With these open wounds, God would use my life to walk closely with the Evans family in ways that I never walked before. For this grace, I will always be grateful.

The amount of loss in our family in such a short time was staggering. Every one of these losses was painful for me, but losing Wynter was, of course, the hardest of all. But these passings served as an up close and personal reminder that death is something that every one of us must face someday. It's a reality that affects each of us, and no one is exempt. There is a beauty when death is close because it reminds you of its reality. And somehow, when you start to think about it more realistically, you begin to think about life a little differently.

Solomon spoke of this beauty when he said, "It is better to go to a house of mourning than to go to a house of feasting, for death is the destiny of everyone; the living should take this to heart" (Ecclesiastes 7:2).

Many people think of death as a final destination, and then they live their lives as if they were never going to die. But the Bible tells us that there is a life beyond this life and offers us the promise of the home we have always wanted to find. That home is our promised land, and every day we step a little closer to it.

In his letter to the Corinthians, the apostle Paul urged followers of Jesus, and anyone that would listen, to remember that someday our earthly body would pass away. His words are a call to take an inventory of our lives, as we consider how we might point others to the One that Paul and every Christian has discovered—Jesus, Savior and Lord of all:

> Therefore we are always confident and know that as long as we are at home in the body we are away from the Lord. For we live by faith, not by sight. We are confident, I say, and would prefer to be away from the body and at home with the Lord (2 Corinthians 5:6-8).

This life is not all there is. It is easy, Paul is saying, for us to mistake this present world for our home. But it is only a temporary waystation on our journey to the place where we will be with God forever.

A week after Lois died, Dr. Evans stood in the pulpit and made a statement that I will never forget: "If you aren't a Christian, then earth is all the heaven you will ever get. But if you are a Christian, then earth is all the hell you will ever get."

During Wynter's funeral, which he helped to officiate, he shared that there was no answer to the question about why such things happen. Sometimes it may feel like God wasn't there when we needed Him most. That He was absent or that He made a bad call. But as Jesus said to Martha, "I am the resurrection and the life. The one who believes in me will live, even though they die" (John 11:25). Jesus, assured Dr. Evans, never makes a mistake, and he paraphrased from the Bible: "We sorrow but not as those who have no hope" (1 Thessalonians 4:13). The pain of loss is understandable, but our loss is not the end of the story.

Wynter was a gift to me, but Jesus and His promise is an even greater gift. And He is the gift that means that someday I will see her again.

6

A SONG FOR MY CHILDREN

I cannot imagine anything harder than telling your children that their amazing mother is gone. As I pulled myself away from Wynter's lifeless body, I knew that the next thing I must do was to help my girls deal with this new reality in their life. I had no time to really process what I was going to say as I was ushered into the sterile little room where they had been kept waiting to hear how their mom was doing. They'd been playing a game with her only a couple hours earlier, and now I had to tell them she had died. I knew they weren't fully prepared for what was to come.

I knew we were loved by the swiftness of the response of those who had come to join us at the hospital. Aunts, uncles, cousins, and friends had been looking after the girls while the battle to save Wynter's life was unfolding. But now it was up to me. In God's kindness, He had allowed Dr. Evans to arrive before this crucial moment, so he joined me in the room. I could not have imagined a more reassuring presence to be with me at that time. He had guided me in my faith walk, and I was gifted to have him as the ideal coach to be alongside me as I talked with my daughters. I knew that every word mattered, as well as my body language and my tone. They would be reading every expression as they listened to me. I don't honestly remember everything I said, but I believe

God gave me the words they needed to hear. I asked them to look me in the eye so they could see my resolve. I wanted them to own the truth that was boiling over in me at that very moment. So, I got down on one knee and told them what I believed with every ounce of my being. It was truth that I had held onto all my life and now could lean into in this difficult moment of pain. I wanted them to know that their mommy hadn't just ceased to exist. Even the thought of them thinking that angered me.

"Mommy went home to be with Jesus."

Simple words, yes, but the only words I knew would help them navigate this crisis. And the only true words that were necessary. They were as shocked and heartbroken as I was. Words really can't describe the anguish, confusion, and pain that entered into that room. An unexpected death feels so strange. Mostly, we just held each other and cried.

Trying to help them find the confidence I had been given by God, I began to sing "Good Good Father" over them.

There, during the hardest moment of my entire life, I knew that I needed to remind the girls of the goodness of God and the security of His love. As I sang, we sought God's comfort together. I could not protect them from the pain of losing their mom, a woman who had poured everything she had into their lives. But I knew I could invite them to join me in a unity of Spirit like that Paul referred to in his letter to the church at Philippi:

> Therefore if you have any encouragement from being united with Christ, if any comfort from his love, if any common sharing in the Spirit, if any tenderness and compassion, then make my joy complete by being like-minded, having the same love, being one in the spirit and of one mind (Philippians 2:1-2).

I knew that it would be a work of the Spirit that would bring us through this time. And I knew it would be our unity that would give us strength for the days to come. That moment was the beginning of a level of unity that my family continues to fight for through all our adversity. Through many trials, God has been kind to continue to keep us like-minded in our trust in Him.

As I was delivering the news to my girls, the medical team removed all the equipment that had been attached to Wynter, and cleaned her up, prettied her hair, and placed her in a small, comfortable room so that everyone who wanted to could say goodbye. They encouraged me to spend a few last minutes with her, and as I entered the room, I saw her small, fragile body lying there helpless and covered by a clean sheet. I saw her fuzzy blue socks, which she loved so much, poking out from the sheet. I couldn't help it. A little grin burst forth on my face at the sight of those little socks which she wore so often, a sign that she was comfortable and "at home." Her body looked as restful as she did when she slept. She was as beautiful as ever. And so peaceful.

After spending a few minutes alone with her, I invited the family members to come into the room. By now there were dozens of them in the lobby. We all found places around the bed, all of us still shocked at the unexpected events of the past few hours. It had all happened so fast. None of us really had words to express what we were feeling, so I leaned back on what had brought me a measure of peace, asking Priscilla to lead us in a song. She thought just a moment, and then began to softly sing a classic hymn of hope, "Victory in Jesus."

Priscilla is a gifted singer, and as the rich and beautiful tone of her voice filled the room, hope came flooding in. Through her tears and gut-wrenching agony, Priscilla was leaning on what she knew to be true. Though death was present in the room in the small body of my beloved Wynter, the words Priscilla sang were pointing to the eternal life that had broken through. Death would not swallow up Wynter. She was now in the hands of her Savior.

> When the perishable has been clothed with the imperishable, and the mortal with immortality, then the saying that is written will come true: "Death has been swallowed up in victory. Where, O death, is your victory? Where, O death, is your sting?" The sting of death is sin, and the power of sin is the law. But thanks be to God! He gives us the victory through our Lord Jesus Christ (1 Corinthians 15:54-57).

7

SURROUNDED

Within an hour or two of Wynter's passing, the people that she had loved the most dropped everything to be with us, to be there for our family. They became the hands and feet and voice of Jesus, ministering to us, serving us, and mostly, just loving us.

We were surrounded by love.

Our friends Val Gorman and her husband, Greg, were among the first on the scene. I was told by the paramedics that we were initially routed to a rather run-down medical center, but we had been miraculously rerouted to the much newer hospital where Val happened to work as a surgeon. Their family understood emergencies. Val greeted me with a long hug as I awaited news of Wynter's condition, and then helped take charge of getting the information on her status to me. Her husband, Greg, arrived about ten minutes later as I was sitting in a chair outside the room, trying to compose myself. He leaned over, tenderly kissed me on the forehead, and started to pray for Wynter and for me and for the girls. His presence was just the gift I needed at that moment.

It would be Val— a dear friend of Wynter—who would speak some of the most impactful words into our family. I wasn't there to hear it, but what she said to my oldest daughter Alena gave her the strength to bring her through this moment. This is how Alena shared it the day after her mommy went home to be with the Lord. It shows her remarkable wisdom and understanding at a moment of immense pain and hurt.

@alenapitts

On July 24, 2018, Jesus took my precious mommy off this earth. It happened within a couple hours and was so sudden. My heart hurts like never before. Comfort seems far. Anxiety is extremely present. It still feels like a dream that I will wake up from soon. I will remember those thirty minutes for the rest of my life. And I will remember the pain I felt as I found out. But the nurse [Val Gorman, who was actually the surgeon] repeated this phrase to me as I walked down that hospital hallway. And for some reason I couldn't forget these words. As they told me my mom had passed, these words continued and still continue to pound in my head: "I'm gonna tell you something I need you never to forget, ok? You serve a big God. A big God. Don't you ever forget that." I serve a big God. Obstacles will be thrown at me, but God is still there. He knows what He's doing and He's got a plan. I say this not by sheer will but through faith. In the moment, His plan may seem outrageous and I may not understand. I continue to ask myself, "Why me?" Why did He choose my family? But I'm reminded He's in control. Even as I weep and grieve, I can smile with joy because I'll see her again. Even now she's been throwing little winks at me. Please be praying for my family as my three younger sisters and I have lost our mommy, and dad has lost his best friend.

———

Dr. Evans was there with his pastoral presence and air of authority. He is a man with unique spiritual gifts—a giant. To have him there felt like having a powerful and comforting blanket of protection covering us. Other than my own father, who was more than a thousand miles away, there wasn't another man on earth I would more have wanted by my side as I shared the news with my girls.

Also present were Wynter's "sister cousins," as she called them—Dr. Evans's daughters Priscilla and Crystal, as well as his daughter-in-law, Kanika. Wynter's brother's wife, Andrea, the closest thing to a real sister she had ever known, was also there with us. Having these amazing women present with us provided some small sense of normalcy and comfort to the girls, a quiet assurance that though they had lost their mother, this team of surrogate mothers stood at the ready for them. And to this day, each has, in her own way, stepped up to plug holes and fill gaps with complete joy in her heart for the opportunity.

Wynter's big brother, Sean, was there. He was in shock at the news but remained steady in his trust in God's faithfulness. I was so moved when, at the funeral, he stood to say that he had lost a sister but had gained a brother in the process. He is a guy who usually doesn't say much, so these words were especially powerful for me. Though never one to show a lot of emotion, he is always there when I need him— faithful, generous, and consistent. He is the best "brother from another mother" that any guy could have.

Throughout the hours and days and weeks and months that have passed, so many people have been there for me and the girls. Not for a single moment did I ever feel alone in my pain and loss…and neither did my girls. I know that not everyone has the blessing of being surrounded by such love and care, but I am forever grateful for those who were present at the moment we needed them most, and never failed to be there later as we began to process our grief one moment at a time.

In the middle of the worst kind of pain, we need each other. And more than each other, we desperately need our loving God. I simply can't imagine living life without deep and rich relationships in my life. There have been many, but none have sustained me more or given me more strength than my friendship with Jesus.

He reminds each of us, "I am the vine; you are the branches. If you remain in me and I in you, you will bear much fruit; apart from me you can do nothing" (John 15:5). Oh, the difference it makes when we are attached to Him as a grape is to a vine.

I knew these words to be true up until this point in my life. But when my trust was being tested most in these dark days, I learned this truth experientially. God was teaching me. It wasn't just good theology. It was life. I had attached myself to Him, and it was in these moments of pain that I felt His presence and His life-giving sustenance most deeply.

8

EXIT STRATEGY

When we entered the hospital, it was just before sundown, but now, as we piled into the car to drive away, it was dark. And with the darkness, a feeling of despair fell over me.

I've never felt anything like what I experienced that first evening. Leaving the hospital, I felt like I was abandoning Wynter, leaving her there all alone, cold and unprotected. We had gently removed her fuzzy blue socks. She had always counted on her fuzzy socks and a warm blanket to soothe her soul when she felt afraid, intimidated, or insecure. Now I needed them more than she did.

Instead of returning to the house where we had been staying—which I simply couldn't face—we found ourselves at my brother-in-law's home. His place seemed like a secure refuge as we let the storm pass over us. This was a place where we had shared Christmases, where the girls had danced and laughed and giggled. But now the house was filled with a strange quiet. I think we all felt helpless and hopeless, despite my earlier sense of peace.

As I settled into a comfy chair, I remembered the question posed early that morning by an incoming blog: Do you have an exit strategy? I needed something to distract me from thinking about Wynter, so I opened up the blog post and read it. I was expecting an article that would address leadership and transitions, but instead it contained words of hope addressed to Christians in the face of death. These words from Randy Frazee were so good that I read them aloud to the family right then and there. It was a surprise gift from God to encourage me and those that would join me that evening.

Here is what it said:

> My first experience with waterskiing came at the age of twenty-four. I was quietly anxious about the adventure. All of my focus was on getting up on those skis. The first attempt was over before it began. One tug from the motorboat, and the rope left my hands and took off without me. On the second try, I got up for a brief second before I faceplanted and a rush of brown lake water was sent up my nose. On the third attempt I kept the tension just right to bring my body out of the water. As my body fully emerged, I leaned back just a bit and found the slot. I did it! I was water skiing. A smile overtook my entire face. I had accomplished the goal! Check.
>
> Then it dawned on me. I had spent all my energy and focus on my entrance strategy and had invested zero time considering my exit strategy. I had no idea how to end this experience. Fear overtook me. Thoughts of my falling body skipping across the water like a smooth stone came to mind. Thoughts of my legs rising above my head as I made contact with the concrete water below elevated my blood pressure.
>
> So, I held on for dear life as the boat continued circling the small lake. The guys on the boat began to yell out something to me, but I couldn't quite make it out. By this time my hands and legs were cramping. How was this going to end? It had to end. I couldn't hold on forever. I yelled for the guys to speak louder.
>
> They screamed at the top of their lungs, "Let go of the rope!"
>
> Let go of the rope? They must be insane. What happens to a body that just lets go of the rope and gives up? I didn't

know, because I had never experienced it before. So, I doubled down on my grip and kept skiing, completely unsure of how it was all eventually going to end.

Life is so often like my waterskiing adventure. We use all of our energy getting up and staying up but don't have an exit strategy. We know we can't continue the ride forever in this body—it will eventually give out—but, because we don't know how the ride ends and fear it will hurt, we hold on for dear life.

Woody Allen said, "I don't mind dying; I just don't want to be there when it happens." Boy, can I relate!

What is the exit strategy for the Christian? If I said yes to Christ in this life, what happens to me when I die, when I let go of the rope?

The Bible has so much to say about this that will calm your nerves, loosen your death grip on life and give you hope. Consider the words of Paul in his letter to the Corinthian believers—

> Therefore we do not lose heart. Though outwardly we are wasting away, yet inwardly we are being renewed day by day. For our light and momentary troubles are achieving for us an eternal glory that far outweighs them all. So we fix our eyes not on what is seen, but on what is unseen, since what is seen is temporary, but what is unseen is eternal. For we know that if the earthly tent we live in is destroyed, we have a building from God, an eternal house in heaven, not built by human hands—2 Corinthians 4:16–5:1.

Daily our bodies are wasting away. Can I get an "amen"? This is just a fact of life. But as we grow in Christ, Paul says, our spirits can actually get stronger. The second-best for overcoming the effects of aging is diet and exercise. The first-best strategy is spiritual growth, getting healthy on the inside.

We should do everything we can to take care of our bodies (1 Corinthians 6:19-20), but eventually, time takes its toll. I am working hard to slow the process down, but I cannot stop it. I'm not only getting older, but I am getting shorter. Somewhere between high school and now, I have lost an inch off my height. Yikes.

Death will eventually win over these perishable bodies we inherited from Adam, but as we grow spiritually and get to know God better, we will see he has a plan for us. His plan trumps all the pain and even physical death we experience in this life. It's a plan where love wins and we live forever. On the day of Christ's return we will receive a new body, a resurrected body that is imperishable. When we fix our eyes on this promise it makes the temporary troubles we have in life now seem puny in comparison. Because no matter how awful our circumstances become, we know this is not how our story ends. We will receive relief from our grief one day. The believer in Jesus can cope with this hope.

That summer day when I was waterskiing so many years ago, I finally did it. I let go of the ski rope. What happened? My body slowly sank into the water. The life jacket kept me afloat as the boat circled around to pick me up. Everything was fine. And the next time out I not only had an entrance strategy but an exit strategy.

Death, the Bible tells us, is a valley experience. But at some point in the valley, Jesus will meet us there and take us the rest of the way (see Psalm 23:4). Death is a sting. But, the sting is only temporary. Once it wears off and is over, you are left with eternity in the presence of God. Whenever it is time for you to let go of the rope of life, you will discover that everything will be just fine. No, not fine…better than ever.[2]

—◦◦◦—

As I finished reading these words and put down my phone, there wasn't, as they say, a dry eye in the place. We'd all been incredibly moved by Randy Frazee's words, which so applied to our own situation now. God had an exit strategy for Wynter. When the time came, she just let go of the rope and entered into glory. A powerful reminder that death doesn't have the final word.

Frazee's words spoke so eloquently of the kind of vulnerability we all need to have in the face of death. And God had placed these words in my inbox just hours before I would need them most. All I could think of was, "How kind is our God."

My girls and I settled into my brother-in-law's guest room to try to get some rest. I lay down on the bed and searched my heart for what to say to my precious daughters. I was looking for words of encouragement and comfort, but just couldn't find anything to say that didn't sound hollow.

So, I did what I had done earlier in the hospital. I sang.

And as I lifted my voice in various songs of worship that were familiar to them, one by one they joined in. Our worship was from our hearts, though it wasn't born out of gladness, but out of desperation and anguish. We needed God. And we needed each other. And we knew that we were united in our love for Him.

We started singing, and in a very real sense, we have never stopped.

The girls all climbed on the bed, and they lay across my body. Their weight felt like a comforting blanket of security covering me. It was a reminder of the weight that would carry me through the first difficult year of grieving: the weight of responsibility. Now it was I alone who would carry the responsibility of caring for them—or at least, so I thought.

I remembered the words I had spoken to Wynter, among the very last words I had shared with her: "I will take care of the girls, babe. You don't have to worry about them."

9

THE ROAD AHEAD

Before we settled in Tennessee, and before our final days in Texas, we had spent only four nights in our new home. Then came a brief trip to Iowa to visit my family and celebrate my grandmother's ninety-fourth birthday. Everybody was there—my parents, my siblings, their spouses, my mom's mom, as well as me, my girls, some more extended family, and Wynter. In God's kindness, one of my sisters had lined up a photo shoot with a professional photographer. That photo shoot was exactly a week before Wynter passed from death into life. These pictures would be the last ones to include Wynter, and they are a precious gift to me even today.

Then, Wynter and our oldest daughter, Alena, flew to a conference in San Antonio, a special gathering for girls of all ages. Alena had become a very gifted speaker and singer, so she joined her mom in ministering to this large group of girls and their moms. By nature, Wynter was a homebody, but God had been opening doors for her to speak all over the country. She learned to put up with the difficulties of living out of a suitcase and the unexpected detours and delays of the traveling life. In many ways, I know it wouldn't have been her choice, but she had a passion for helping girls and knew God was using her in this way. Very soon her speaking had become as powerful as her writing, and she was beginning to be in demand.

As she and Alena flew to San Antonio, the other three girls joined me for a long drive south from the Iowa cornfields to the sprawling neighborhoods of north Texas. It was strange to have the passenger seat empty for the long and boring drive, but I was beaming inside with a pride for all that Wynter was accomplishing. While the girls watched movies in the back of the van, I listened to sermons and podcasts and talk shows discussing the country's future. But it didn't seem the same without her.

This long road trip was a precursor of my road ahead. Without even noticing it, I would typically wrap my right arm inside of Wynter's left bicep, with my palm resting on the back of her forearm, which was on her armrest. On this trip, she wasn't there to connect with, and I missed it. I would soon learn how much. I wouldn't feel complete without her there beside me.

―――∽∞∽―――

Throughout my life, I have never really been alone. I am a textbook extrovert, always happiest when surrounded by others. I grew up with an identical twin, Ben, who was my companion from day one. We shared a bedroom, sports teams, classes in school, and our very DNA. I never knew what personal space was or cared about having it. When I went to college, I became fast friends with my roommate, Geoff. We roomed together throughout our college days, most of them sharing a bedroom. And then I married Wynter just two weeks after college graduation, and she became my wife and my constant companion for the next 15 years of my life.

Now she was gone. But her scents and perfumes remained, permeating our bedroom and bathroom. All around me were the clothes she loved so much and that looked so lovely on her, as well as all the shoes she had purchased over the years. Wynter wasn't particularly good at keeping them all organized, but now I was grateful for the clutter. It helped me sense her presence every time I entered the room.

It's taken me time to detach from some of these items. I'll be forever grateful for how the Lord allowed my senses to slowly let go of Wynter.

She left suddenly, but her presence left more slowly as I learned to trust her into the arms of her Perfect Husband. Her passing has given me much more insight into an aspect of God—His husbandry. I was a good husband, but He is the Perfect Husband. Trusting His perfect love for her, I could begin to let her go.

> For your Maker is your husband;
> his name is Yahweh, Commander of Angel Armies!
> Your Kinsman-Redeemer is the Holy One of Israel!
> He has the title Mighty God of All the Earth!
> 　(Isaiah 54:5 TPT).

The nights were the hardest. I was overcome by a sense of cold darkness, as if the primary thing that had lit up my life had been snuffed out. In the dark, my mind wandered to picturing her, laid out lifeless in a cold, dark morgue. I worried about her alone there…and about myself alone here. One minute, all was normal and we were together and in love. The next minute, she had slipped away from me. The nights and the darkness of death were the worst for me. And when daylight broke, I would find myself more hopeful again.

For a Christian, this is the reality of grieving. You find moments where it is possible to live with a confident trust that God has it all in His hands. Then, a moment later, the fear and the doubts and the questionings come crowding into your mind. That is what I experienced. Trust in the middle of the deepest bewilderment. Bewilderment in the middle of the most fervent trust.

The first couple of nights, I would lie awake in the dark, unable to slip away into sleep, my heart beating out of control and my eyes wide in the gloom of midnight

One moment, I would be filled with gratitude for my Wynter season, that we had so many wonderful years together, filled with a joy that had been forged and fought for. The next, I was overwhelmed by all that had transpired in a few short hours, and the deepest sort of sadness settled around my heart. I was on an emotional roller coaster, and not by choice.

Through it all, even when I couldn't seem to feel the comfort, I knew that the Comforter was with me. I thought often of Psalm 34:7, a verse God had given to me as a gift: "The angel of the LORD encamps around those who fear him, and he delivers them." I was usually able to trust in that protective love, though sometimes the enemy of my soul seemed intent upon hijacking my mind.

I didn't want to be alone. I didn't want to be in the dark. And fear sometimes gnawed at me, like a dog on a bone.

I recalled the distinct sense that at the very moment when Wynter died, her soul, her very essence, had left her body. She was there one moment, then she was gone, leaving only a shell that looked like her behind. Deep inside, I knew exactly where she had gone. Of that I was confident. But I was still brokenhearted. In that space, I learned the truth of Psalm 34:18: "The LORD is close to the brokenhearted and saves those who are crushed in spirit." At first, I couldn't find much comfort in this verse, especially when I heard it again and again from well-meaning friends. It sounded a little false, like just the sort of thing you thought you *should* say. But in the weeks that followed, I found that described exactly what I was feeling—that my heart was broken into pieces. It also described the truth that was constant—the feeling of closeness to Jesus that I would hang onto for dear life. And His closeness was most manifest through the closeness of others.

10

TWO BROTHERS

Whenever we go through something traumatic, it's then that we really need each other the most. And God reaches out to us with His love and comfort, most often through the hands of the people in our life—our family and our friends. The greatest joy I've found since Wynter's passing is realizing the depth of the friendships I have, that Wynter had, and that we had together.

I made it through the darkest part of this journey because I could hold on to Jesus and because my family and friends held on to me. What was true on the evening when Wynter died, so it is true today. I am surrounded.

When Wynter died, Ben was living in southern New Jersey, only a few towns over from where we had grown up together. When I went to college in Philadelphia, he enrolled at West Point Military Academy. By the time he returned home, I had married Wynter and moved to Texas. Because of the distance that separated us, we only got to see each other in person two or three times a year, but it wasn't unusual for us to talk on the phone just about every day. Despite the distance, we stayed close.

As soon as Ben got the news, he bought a plane ticket for the next available flight. Once he was in Texas, he didn't leave my side for ten days. Sean and Andrea, with whom we were staying, managed to figure out a way to squeeze another person into their home. They knew I needed to be with my brother. The two of us crashed each night on an air mattress in the living room—tucked together like we probably were in the womb—because the house was so full of family members. Somehow, his very presence helped me find a little peace and sleep more soundly. Even his breathing and snoring were a reminder that I wasn't alone.

My brother had always been my protector. Of the two of us, he was the tough one. In middle school, there were at least two fights that I started with others, but in both cases, he was the one who finished them. I should mention he also got suspended taking on my punishment. Ben always looked after my best interests, whether it was warning me against bad relationships or the lure of narcotics. I so depended upon his strength and wisdom that it took a little while after marriage to break free of too much dependence. Leaving and cleaving isn't just about your parents; it can apply to a twin sibling as well! It took us a couple years to figure out how to relate to each other in healthy ways after I was married, but we got there.

Now, when I needed him most, he stepped right back into the role of my protector. He dropped everything going on in his busy life and came to be with me. I'm so grateful that his wife, Leslie, and their three kids understood how much I needed him in those days. I'll always be grateful for that.

Ben was a source of God's love and a light for me in those darkest days. His very presence brought warmth into the coldest of nights. I could sleep easier knowing that God had brought him to "encamp" with me on that inflatable mattress and watch over me. We had been together in the womb, camped side by side in our scouting tents, and now he was here again, beside me on that inflatable mattress. Our bed was like a little raft keeping me afloat in the midst of the waves that had rocked my world.

I'll never forget waking up in the middle of the night in those days before the funeral, gripped with fear. It was then that the simple touch of Ben and the warmth of his humanity would grant me just enough comfort to relax again. I'd breathe easier and sleep more deeply, even if it was only a short time before I'd wake again and settle close to him.

My other brother during the days that followed was a brother by marriage—Anthony Evans, the son of Tony Evans. While Ben was making his way from the East Coast, Anthony was boarding a plane from the West Coast—California. It was like God was surrounding me with a forcefield to have these two men surrounding, protecting, and caring for me.

I first became aware of Anthony because of his musical gifts. He's an amazing vocalist who has spent years of his life using his pipes to give people a rich encounter with the Spirit of God. While we were still in college in Philadelphia, Wynter and I went to see her "cousin" during his tour with Grammy-award-winning musician and producer Kirk Franklin. It was an inspiring and hope-filled night (in fact, the name of the tour was "Hopeville"), and I never could have guessed the role that Anthony would play in my life. When we moved to Texas, we got to know each other better, and we connected immediately, like we had known one another forever. I started traveling with him during his solo tour, helping with the merchandise table and whatever else was needed. But that role as road manager would blossom into serving as his manager for more than seven years. We developed a deep bond and a friendship. We went through a lot together.

I'll always remember those days of traveling from venue to venue and from church to church. We went everywhere: from the apple orchards of Connecticut to the beaches of south Florida and from the towering landscapes of northern California to the low, sandy tundra of the Southwest. In addition to all the beauty I saw, I also learned about the amazing diversity in the body of Christ. We are different, and we are one. Anthony has paid me the greatest of compliments time and time again by sharing with others that his career was built on my ability to build trusting relationships wherever we went—a gift that later came in handy when I went to work for Dr. Tony Evans. I owe Anthony so much. He always encouraged Wynter and me to stretch ourselves. He taught me how to take beneficial risks and to learn to trust my instincts.

As soon as his feet hit the ground in Dallas, Anthony swept into action, helping me manage my life during a time when it was hard to think straight. I was starting to get overwhelmed by everyone's suggestions about how the funeral should be conducted, so he looked me in the eye and told me to quit worrying about everyone's opinions. What I needed to do, he told me, was simply create the funeral that the girls and I wanted. I'd been creating such stress for myself by trying to work around everyone else's schedules and plans and proposals, so Anthony's words were like a weight being lifted off my shoulders.

He stepped in and took care of a lot of the other details and managed the logistics of planning a "Celebration of Life" for Wynter with all the energy he put into producing one of his own live productions. I could rest easy knowing he was in control. One thing you learn when you lose someone you love is that there are a lot of people seeking to make a profit off your loss. They know you are vulnerable, and they will often guide you to spend more money than you need to. Anthony took care of this kind of stuff for me and let me focus on my grief and my daughters.

Then, once the funeral was past, Anthony came out to Franklin, Tennessee, to help us set up our new house there. We had barely unpacked during the four days that we were in Tennessee prior to traveling, and Anthony instinctively went into overdrive. He knew the importance of aesthetics and comfort, so he went out of his way to make sure that our house was a home. He bought furniture and knick-knacks on his own dime, never sharing receipts or details with me. He arranged the furniture. He took the girls to school. He ordered dinner, and he made breakfast.

At one point, he told me to create a digital folder of all my favorite pictures of Wynter and our family. Days later, a large box arrived with each of these pictures beautifully framed in different sizes, including my favorite—a large portrait of Wynter—that now hangs in a collage of family memories running up the staircase.

For the first year after her passing, I would kiss her on the lips every time I passed that large portrait. In fact, I still do that sometimes as a symbol of our enduring love. Anthony even helped me create a little memorial of her for our main hallway—a gathering of photos lined up on a little wooden bench with a few pillows, one with a large *W*. It's a reminder for all of us of the special woman Wynter will always be to us.

Anthony was with us for a number of days, meeting whatever needs might arise, but the greatest gift he gave was his presence. Just having him there in those incredibly painful first days put me more at ease and made me feel worthy. He served me beyond my ability to ever pay him back, and for that I'm forever grateful.

11

FRIENDS

The people who had already been part of our lives rallied to our side. They were people God had already made part of our world before we even knew how much we'd eventually need them. They were already deeply involved in our lives, but our tragedy drew them even closer.

One such person was Nicole Staples, who was among Wynter's closest friends. They had met when Nicole offered to do a free photo shoot of the girls. In fact, our family was her first shoot after she moved from Florida to Texas in 2011. Interestingly, one of the photos from that session became the cover for the first issue of *For Girls Like You,* Wynter's magazine for tween girls. This beautiful cover remains, for me, a symbol of the love that developed between Wynter and Nicole. And it all started with a gift—a free photo session.

As the magazine took off, the two of them were able to bring their own talents to the table: Wynter for writing, and Nicole for design. Helping the magazine excel in both these areas became the foundation for both a growing friendship and creating a high-quality outreach to young girls. I'd often come home from work and find the two of them wrapped up in blankets, lounging on the couch with their hands encircling cups of coffee, strategizing how to make this the most beautiful magazine it could be—accompanied by lots of laughing, dreaming, and planning.

Because Nicole was single, we grafted her into our family. She became a younger sister to me and a big sister to our girls. When Wynter and I needed a little time for just the two of us, Nicole would offer to come and watch the girls. The girls loved her, and it was very hard for them when we had to say goodbye to her in preparation for the move to Tennessee.

I can't remember exactly what Nicole was doing during the week after Wynter's passing, but I can tell you one thing: She was present. She was there with us in our time of need, an almost constant comfort to the girls, and working hard on gathering photos for the memorial service. No fuss, no drawing attention to herself, just doing what needed to be done.

My friendship with Nicole grew in the months that followed. She was there at our first Thanksgiving dinner without Wynter and she celebrated New Year's Eve with my three youngest girls, which they were thrilled about. For the latter, she came up with the idea of having my three youngest write a sweet note to their mommy, attaching them to balloons, and then releasing them into the Dallas skyline from the top of her loft—the loft that Wynter helped her choose just a few years prior. As the fireworks celebrated the New Year, it marked a new season in all our lives. And she wanted the girls to remember that their mommy in heaven would continue to be part of their lives.

Now, Nicole is a critical part of carrying on Wynter's work and legacy through *For Girls Like You Ministries*. Her energy and creativity have been a huge part of the continuing success of Wynter's vision. At first, she volunteered, but her gifts would continue to make way for her growth within a rapidly expanding organization. For the first year and a half after Wynter's passing, I led like a man who knew that failing wasn't an option, but I soon realized I was depleting myself. The subscription base was growing, and so were the responsibilities! In no time at all, Nicole became the backbone of the ministry. Her God-given gifts in all the areas of design and project management have proven crucial to our growth. Eventually, she moved to Tennessee to take over as the full-time director for the ministry, which took everything to the next level. Nicole and Wynter were the best of friends and partners in so many ways, and I know Wynter would be pleased that her legacy is being carried forward by someone who really understands and appreciates what this dream is all about—God's girls.

But even more than that, Nicole is a mentor for my girls and yet another surrogate mother figure who believes in them, encourages them, and even challenges them, just as I know Wynter would want.

Through my ministry contacts, many years ago, I met a couple named John and Suzanne, who ran a mentoring program in one of the rougher neighborhoods of Dallas. Along with teaching life skills, they provided tutoring, meals, clothing, and a lot of love to dozens of amazing yet disadvantaged kids. I was so inspired by the work they were doing that I really wanted Wynter to meet them. When she did, she fell in love with what they were doing, and she fell in love with them. So, we got involved. Once a week we'd load our crew into the minivan and drive into a crime-ridden, drug-infested, and largely forgotten part of Dallas. Not only did we want to help, but we wanted to model this kind of compassion and service to our girls. In no time at all, our girls were making friends with the kids in that impoverished neighborhood, and we were becoming extended family to those who lived there. We went to serve needs, but we realized we were also there to serve as a positive model of what a family can be. It was humbling and sometimes intimidating, but always incredibly life giving. I saw Wynter's big heart expand even more as she led a girls' group, which was a great place to test the materials she was creating and hear more stories about how God was working in young lives.

It was during these long afternoons of service that we met Kameron Mitchell, a single guy with a heart of compassion and a lot of creativity. This gentle guy had no children of his own, but he treated these, especially the ones without a father, like they were his own. During the four years we volunteered, we built a strong friendship with Kameron. Soon we were not just seeing him in the "neighborhood," but having him to our home and inviting him into our lives.

When that ministry closed its doors, I gave Kameron a job as my assistant at The Urban Alternative. His creativity was a gift to the ministry, and he also used that creativity to help Wynter redesign our bedroom into what she'd always dreamed it might be. When the remodel was finished—ironically, just a few months before we decided to move to Tennessee—he brought two large, black frames in which he placed two words in black print on white matte paper. They carried a simple message: Be Still. One word in each frame. When we first moved to Tennessee, Wynter and I hung those words in the new bedroom in the same spot.

So many times, these words have helped me to deal with my stress and anxiety and overcome the natural tendencies of my personality. They quiet my spirit whenever I feel overwhelmed. What's beautiful is that these words are the very spirit that Wynter embodied during her life. They describe the way she lived.

These words, of course, are from the Bible: "'Be still, and know that I am God; I will be exalted among the nations, I will be exalted in the earth.' The LORD Almighty is with us; the God of Jacob is our fortress" (Psalm 46:10-11).

These words and these scriptures are a reminder that we can trust the God of the Bible. They are an encouragement for us to trust Him and not to think it is up to us and our efforts to solve all our problems. Learning to be still and trust Him to take them makes all the difference.

I find myself even now looking up at those words on my saddest and most stressful days and simply saying, "Jonathan…Be still." I gaze upon them whenever I wonder what God has in my future and need to be reminded that He will never abandon me. And I look to them when I feel overwhelmed by the mantle of leadership I wear for my girls, my church, and for Wynter's ministry.

The Bible is realistic; it never promises that we won't have problems. It only promises that we won't have to face them alone. It encourages us to let them go and not spend all our energy worrying about how everything will turn out. It's as if God is saying, "Relax, I've got this."

Be still.

That little reminder from Kameron spoke to my own situation

over the next months and years. The peace that God gives can see you through whatever storms may arise in your life, just as it did in mine.

—⟨⟨⟨⟨|⟩|⟩⟩⟩⟩—

Another friend, we will call her Meghan, had moved to Texas as a newly wedded wife and was soon the mother of a little girl. Sadly, life took a few unexpected turns, and she ended up a single mom. She and I met professionally. We had lots of good conversations about leadership and hard work, and sometimes we talked about the difficulties she was facing. That's where Wynter came in.

As Wynter got to know her, Meghan opened up about the bitterness and anger she felt after her marriage fell apart and the ugly custody battles that followed. Wynter listened with great sympathy. She could understand what Meghan was going through because she had watched her own mother endure similar trials. She'd had a front-row seat as a daughter who watched her mom take the healthiest path through the pain—trusting Jesus and loving even those who were causing her pain. Wynter's dad had been a drug addict and had put her family in harm's way, but even years later, her mom wouldn't speak bitter or hurtful words about him. As a child, Wynter saw her mother's meekness to be weakness, but she came to discover the power to be found in dispensing grace and walking in humility. There was strength in her approach—a strength that gave her freedom from bitterness and anger and resentment.

Though Meghan's story was very different from Wynter's, she found a quiet wisdom in Wynter's confident and steady approach to life. Wynter became not just a mentor, but a model. And also a dear friend.

As I began writing this book, I asked Meghan what Wynter had meant to her life. This is what she told me:

> The one thing that I most vividly remember was one night when we were all sitting around your kitchen table. I was sharing all my frustrations and the ways I had been wronged. I remember Wynter simply saying, "Meghan,

have grace with him. I know it is hard right now, but you'll get through this with grace." These words are still on repeat in my brain. It seems like the simplest thing to say, but it spoke volumes to me. I needed to hear it, even if at the time I don't think I really wanted to hear it. But Wynter knew I needed it. That one conversation changed my perspective from being broken and hurt to being in a state of healing. To this day, I find myself repeating her words in my head.

Wynter's words are a perfect reflection of the kind of person she sought to be. Loving, caring, compassionate, and filled with grace, as well as straightforward and no nonsense. I think this combination of qualities explain why she had such an impact on the many lives she touched.

Like Nicole and like Kameron, Meghan set up a temporary camp of protection and care around my daughters. In that season, I don't remember all she did, but she was present. She had a servant's heart, and despite the continuing challenges of her own life, she was fully there for us when we needed her most. She shared with us the kind of light that she had received from Wynter. Just as Wynter had invested in her, she invested in my girls with her time and her lighthearted conversation in the times they needed it most. She and her daughter continue to hold an incredibly special place in our hearts. They remind us that God's blessings in relationships are never one-sided, but always mutually beneficial.

12

JEHOVAH JIREH

It seemed like God had a different role for each person who stepped in to help me and the girls through the days and months that followed Wynter's death. Another person who made a big difference in our lives was Wynter's cousin Chrystal, another of Dr. Evans's daughters. During the course of our marriage, Chrystal had become like a big sister to me. Her practicality and her pragmatism came in very handy when we were trying to navigate the changes in our lives.

When she unexpectedly found herself a single mom while in college, Chrystal determined to press ahead with her plans and not let a single decision destroy her future. She stayed the course and graduated with a degree in accounting despite all the challenges she faced, and she has made a good home for her husband, her kids, and her blended family—two daughters and three sons. Chrystal knows how to multitask. She somehow manages to homeschool the kids, bake bread and take care of her home, write books, and speak at conferences all over the US.

In the middle of her ultra busy life, Chrystal dropped everything when her "sister cousin" died. She put her own grief aside and helped us tackle many of the practical issues we had to deal with in the days that followed, one of the biggest being the financial challenges that I couldn't even begin to process. Because Wynter had a heart murmur and a blood-clotting disorder, the only life insurance that would cover her was prohibitively expensive. All we carried was a minimal policy through my own insurance carrier at work. And it barely covered the funeral expenses.

Chrystal was inspired by an idea and got to work. She knew that we were in a place in our lives where things were going to be financially challenging with only one income now. Without saying a word to me, Chrystal set up and published a crowd-sourcing fund-raiser for me and the girls. Before I knew anything about it, the campaign had already garnered tens of thousands of dollars in support. When it was all said and done, the social media campaign gathered $120,000, given by over 6,800 people, many of whom didn't even know us but wanted to help out anyway. That campaign reminded me of God's provision and kindness, and it assured me of the immense power of the body of Christ to care for one another. It opened my eyes to the level of care that people had for Wynter, my girls, and me.

This amazing generosity made such a difference in helping us resettle in Tennessee and get our footing. It helped pay off a large student debt that Chrystal didn't even know existed and allowed me to pay down some other outstanding debts. What is really amazing is that Chrystal didn't really know anything about our financial situation. She just acted in obedience on a prompting from the Holy Spirit. The Lord used her as an angel of mercy in a time of great need, and it gave me one less thing to worry about during a time that already had more than enough stresses. Unless you've been through it, most people don't realize the financial burdens that accompany the loss of a loved one.

Chrystal's actions were the method of God's provision for that season in our life. Both Wynter and I came from less than middle income earning homes. As a result we graduated from college with a lot of debt. There was no family inheritance or financial surplus to help us through. It meant the early years were pretty lean, and money was always an issue. Still, we always prioritized investing into the work of God's Kingdom. It was a commitment we made and a commitment we kept. We gave to God first, even in the leanest of times. We understood that every dime we had was from the Lord, and so we honored Him with our tithe. We trusted the promise of Proverbs: "Honor the

Lord with your wealth, with the firstfruits of all your crops; then your barns will be filled to overflowing, and your vats will brim over with new wine" (Proverbs 3:9-10).

Let me be clear. We didn't give so that we could get. We didn't have the attitude that God owed us anything. We just knew that we owed everything to Him, and that He would take care of us. He did. We never really had any excess in our early years together, but we always had enough. And time and time again, God surprised us with blessings we could never have afforded.

For years, we invested in the Kingdom beyond what most financial planners would probably recommend. While most couples were concerned with maxing out their 401(k)s, we were "emptying our barns" through giving to the church and to people in need. It was the best kind of investment. We didn't look to buy the latest gadgets or a new boat. But that wasn't a burden. It was a blessing.

Then (as the verse promises) when our own need was great, our spiritual ROI (return on investment) was beyond belief. I love the word *then*, which is used in the verse above. It speaks to the reality that God provides at the needed time. Maybe not before, maybe not even after, but during our "then" moment, we can trust that He will show up! During the hardest of seasons, God was showering a very practical blessing down on us. Seeing what God was doing created a tectonic shift in my theology and my understanding of who God was. I began to embrace the truth of His Word more than ever before, and the truth of His love became more real than I had ever experienced it. I understood the reality of God's provision like I never had before. God revealed Himself to me as "Jehovah Jireh," a name given to Him by Abraham which means "the Lord will provide" (see Genesis 22:14).

I'd long known Him as "Jehovah Jireh," but at our moment of greatest need, my eyes were further opened to a God who fills barns "to overflowing" and causes vats to "brim over with new wine." And because of how He helped us—by using our brothers and sisters in Christ—I learned very clearly that our real wealth was in the Kingdom relationships we had built.

In a time of great need, God became more than enough for me. I was living out the words of the apostle Paul to the church at Ephesus: "Now to him who is able to do immeasurably more than all we ask or imagine, according to his power that is at work within us, to him be glory in the church and in Christ Jesus throughout all generations, for ever and ever! Amen" (Ephesians 3:20-21).

Amen indeed.

And now my greatest joy is found in being part of God's Kingdom ROI for those who come across my path. God's abundance isn't just for me, but for those that are just arriving on the doorstep of their "then" moment.

As believers, God is always standing at the door, always knocking on our hearts, always asking if we will be the manifestation of His Jehovah Jireh and "to overflowing" presence for those around us. It is here, in living out this reality, that I really taste the truth of God's Word: "I've left you an example of how you should serve and take care of those who are weak. For we must always cherish the words of our Lord Jesus, who taught, 'Giving brings a far greater blessing than receiving'" (Acts 20:35 TPT).

13

THE DANCE

Just 27 days before she died, Wynter and I celebrated our 15-year wedding anniversary. It was an incredibly special milestone. We didn't have a perfect marriage, but we tried to outdo each other in loving and honoring and serving each other. When we didn't, we sought forgiveness from each other. Those moments, I can assure you, were not uncommon. We weren't perfect, but we were absolutely intentional. Our intentionality was the sign of our love.

I really wanted this anniversary to be special. And I wanted to remind Wynter of the depth of my love for her.

It was a crazy time for us, with all our preparations for the big move to Tennessee consuming so much of our time. Plus, I was incredibly busy at my job as I tied up the loose ends and helped prepare for the transition my leaving would necessitate. Meanwhile, Wynter had the usual pressures of getting together the next issue of the magazine, as well as preparing for some upcoming speaking opportunities. She also had another looming book deadline. It would have been easy just to let this anniversary pass by without too much fanfare. But I was determined not to do that.

In years past, I would often spend a lot of money getting her a special gift that screamed, "I love you!" But over the years, I had learned that this wasn't really what she wanted. What made her happy was to know I was thinking of her and wanting to make her happy. So, I thought at first that maybe a trip for the two of us to Cabo or Aruba would be the perfect way to mark the special day. I had tons of airline and hotel points, so it wouldn't even have been a financial burden. But when I mentioned this possibility, Wynter just shrugged and suggested that she'd rather have the two of us spend some time with the girls. It was as though she somehow sensed that time with the family was the most important thing right now.

So, I was still struggling with finding the perfect gift for her when, driving along and listening to a song by a duo, Caleb and Kelsey, God gave me a spark of inspiration. As I drove, their cover medley of Shania Twain's "From This Moment On/You're Still the One" came floating out of my speakers, and I thought that these were the perfect words to describe how I felt about her…and about us. It was suddenly clear to me. I wanted to dance with Wynter while that song played in the background.

I began to wonder how to make it happen and keep it a surprise. Wynter loved surprises. I contacted Kameron, who is one of the most creative people I know, to help me put something unique together. He asked Nicole and another of our friends, Bree, to help him put together a plan. They did, and they even planned a way to capture the moment on video.

⊸⊸⊸⊸

We started that day with a leisurely drive that ended up at her favorite store in downtown Dallas—a women's clothing shop called Evereve. She loved the place and could always find something that she liked there that would fit her perfectly. Their clothes were elegant, yet modest, and absolutely stunning. Her love for the store had actually started with a seemingly random but fast-growing relationship with the owners, Megan and Mike Tamte. As I watched that day, she tried on several outfits. I posted about the experience on Instagram:

> *All she wants for our 15 year anniversary is to buy a few out-*
> *fits @evereveofficial. So shop we will. :) She has a personal*

shopper and a dressing room with her name on it. I have a
stool, wall backrest, and talk radio in my ears while I wait to
give my opinion on each outfit. Match made in heaven. :) I
love @evereveofficial.

When she was done, we left with a few amazing outfits in hand. She had an ear-to-ear grin that seemed permanent. Nearby was a steak house where I had made reservations, and we shared a tomahawk rib eye that was one of the best we'd ever had. Next up, as far as she knew, was a Netflix movie and a bowl of ice cream in bed, which would have been the perfect ending to a wonderful evening. But I had something else in mind.

Twenty minutes into our drive home, I called Kameron, pretending to be responding to a text he had sent me. We had a discussion about the fact that he had forgotten to turn off the lights at Hampton Estates—a beautiful, white, early-twentieth-century house, which the ministry I worked for had purchased for use as a studio. We had recently restored it to its pristine original splendor. Hampton Estates was located near our home, so I told him I would swing by and take care of it.

As we drove through the gates on that warm June evening, the house was lit up inside, shining magnificently in the growing dark. "Hey," I said to Wynter, "come with me. I don't want to go in there on my own, and I don't want to leave you outside in the car." Since the area surrounding this old estate was a little sketchy, she was happy to agree.

Approaching the house, we could see the beautiful white glow of the chandelier shining through the windows and the glass panes on the front door. Once we were on the porch, with its massive white columns, Wynter peeked inside and saw candlelight, which confused her. Why was there candlelight? An awkward smile of both concern and anticipation sprouted on her face. I took her hand and opened the door.

There was soft, romantic music filling the house. She looked over at me and smiled again. Turning left, we entered the study, where there was a display of desserts and stylish place settings for two arranged around a small table. The room itself was enclosed with built-in bookcases and the original fireplace. The elegance was enough to take your breath away.

"Will you join me for dessert?" I asked gently.

She smiled broadly, a little giddy at the surprise I had created for her. There were cookies and cupcakes and various desserts to choose from, but right in front of her seat were her very favorites—a half-melted cup of Blue Bell Chocolate Chip Cookie Dough ice cream and an old-school bottle of Classic Coke. The ice cream was partially melted because that was the way she liked it best. She'd been known to put a bowl of it in the microwave so that it was both melted and a little warm!

She had no idea what else was coming, but she was basking in the moment. We chatted as we ate our desserts, and then the background music began to fade and finally stopped. Everything was quiet for just a moment, and then the song I had chosen especially for this moment started to play. If you were to check out the lyrics to the song medley, you'd know how perfect it was. Looking back now, I see it as another example of the mystery of God's abundant wisdom and kindness.

I stood, rather formally, and took her hand in mine. "Will you give me this dance?"

She blushed, squeezed my hand, and floated back into the foyer with me.

There is a video of that dance that you can find on YouTube (bit.ly/ PittsAnniversary), which captures the joyfulness and romance of what happened when I took her into my arms as the music started to swell. "Why'd the music get louder?" she asked, but she didn't wait for an answer, moving close to me and adjusting my shirt collar so that she could lean against my shoulder as we danced.

The song spoke of how life began from the moment we met, and how now, after so many years and so many experiences, she is "Still the One" that I love with all my being. My own thoughts were taken up by gratitude. In Wynter, God had given me the greatest of gifts, and in this moment, I wanted her to know. Gratitude for her patience with my failings as a husband. Gratitude for all I had learned from walking this path with her, and gratitude for how her love had changed me.

And now, gratitude for that very moment where we moved together across the floor.

We had made it. Fifteen years. God had done so much in us and through us, and I looked forward to a long future filled with this amazing woman in my life. God had taken an "us" and made it a "we." We were a team, facing every challenge together and celebrating every victory that came our way. We were in a good place. In a good place, together as one.

As the song continued to play, I felt a doubling-down inside myself, stretching my commitment to her to an even greater level. I was excited to see what the next 15 years would hold. We were friends. We were lovers. We were partners together to tackle whatever came our way.

Suddenly, as the song began to wrap up, our daughters, along with our nieces and nephew, made their way down the staircase that rose from the foyer, and they positioned themselves along the banister, each holding a sign. I tried to turn Wynter in such a way as to keep that surprise just a little longer. When "Still the One" began to crescendo, I twirled Wynter around so that she could see the girls and their handwritten messages.

Wynter shrieked with joy and surprise, and I knew that I had sealed the deal. I had achieved what I set out to accomplish. I twirled her back into my arms as we kept dancing until the song finally faded away.

Wynter was overcome with emotion and started to weep quietly, while she whispered into my ear words that will be only ours forever.

The song reminded us of how far we had traveled together to get to the place we were that day. We had made it to this milestone.

I often watch this video of what happened that evening, and it still makes me cry—both in gratitude for all we shared together, and for what I have lost in losing her. I posted it on YouTube so that others could experience a taste of our life together, and so that my girls would always have this special reminder of their mom.

Twenty-seven days later, she would breathe her last on that hospital table, and I would sing to her of my love and God's faithfulness. But that anniversary evening together was about as perfect as anything gets this side of heaven.

14

GOD IS THAT GOOD

I'm one of those people who was raised in a family where there was no question about whether God existed or whether Jesus Christ was the Savior. I don't really remember a time when I didn't believe. Just as surely as my parents fed me plenty of vegetables to maintain my physical health, they fed me on the message of grace: that God loved me and sent Jesus to die for my sins. They wisely helped me to see that following Him was in my best interest and that submitting my life to His Lordship would be the thing that would give my life meaning and fulfillment. But they were never heavy-handed. They never tried to force anything on me. Just as they gently parented me into enjoying a little broccoli or a ripe tomato, so they parented me into taking my place in the Kingdom of God. I'll be forever grateful for that.

I always knew that Garry and Miriam Pitts were looking out for my good, even if I wasn't always happy about every directive I received. And that lent itself to my understanding that God was also always looking out for my good as well.

I learned the truth of Romans 8:28 (NKJV): "All things work together for good to those who love God, to those who are the called according to His purpose." Our world is filled with tragedies, disappointments, evil, and unmet expectations that can make it difficult to arrive at a trust in this truth, but somehow, I did. And through the dark days after losing Wynter, I managed to hold on to this belief. I had seen it in operation throughout my life.

Sometime during high school, I received a leather-bound, maroon New King James Bible as a gift, and that Bible has been my companion through thick and thin. It was there when I felt close to the Lord in seasons of spiritual commitment, and it was there when I struggled against shame and disappointment, especially in my college years.

It's all too easy to begin to question God in the middle of whatever the current struggle might be in our life, but we need the bigger perspective that comes from the pages of the Bible. Every time I read God's Word, I am reminded again that God is good. When I first read this verse, it changed my life. I soon started a habit that I follow to this day. Whenever I was reminded again that this truth lined up with what I was experiencing, I would put a small *x* in the margin of my Bible and record the date. If you were to open up my Bible to this passage today, you'd find dozens and dozens of *x*s and dates recorded there of the significant times in my life when I recognized again that its words were true.

You'd see my wedding date, where it simply reads "JRP to WDE 6/27/2003." A reminder of the day God gave me a gift that was beyond anything I could have dreamed.

You'd find the birthdates of each of my four daughters. With Wynter's health issues, every pregnancy was a step of faith, but each of our girls made their way into the world healthy and whole.

You'd also see the name of my high school mentor, teacher, and coach: Mr. French. He was never afraid to call me out when he needed to. He saw my tendency toward selfishness and gave me the nickname "One Way." (Which, of course, was *my* way!) I didn't appreciate it at the time, but it did me so much good to spend time with him. From him I learned the importance of dying to self, even though I don't ever remember talking to him about God or Jesus in those teenage years.

A few weeks after Wynter died, I received an envelope in the mail, and when I checked the address, I saw it had come from Mr. French. I hadn't seen him in at least ten years. The only thing I had heard is that he had built himself a cabin in the woods of Nebraska, which had been the dream he always talked about. Inside the envelope was a photocopy of a page from the devotional book *Jesus Calling*. It was a devotion for the twenty-ninth of July, which was the date we had buried Wynter. It was a stirring message on endurance, and it included this Scripture passage: "Consider it pure joy, my brothers and sisters, whenever you face trials of many kinds, because you know that the testing of your faith produces perseverance. Let perseverance finish its work so that you may be mature and complete, not lacking anything" (James 1:2-4).

These words were a gift to me on that day, and they had come from a man who had been willing to say the hard things to me as a young man and was now offering words of comfort that were richer than any he could have fashioned himself.

The phrase that had stuck out to me in that devotional was "make every effort." It went on to talk about working to see things from God's perspective—that He is renewing all things and redeeming our deepest pains. It was as if God was spurring me on toward the purposes He had for me, which sadly included this road I would never have chosen to walk. He was encouraging me to welcome it and to walk it with joy— joy beyond my understanding and faith beyond my sight.

———

Those *x*s in my Bible don't just represent the things that were an immediate blessing to my life; they also include remembrances of how God worked for my good even when it didn't feel like it. *X* marks the spot as a reminder that God is good in every circumstance and always has my best in mind. *X* also marks some of the tragedies in my life, like my high school football coach who died very young of Lou Gehrig's disease and my daughter's mentor who never made it to age 30 but died in a car accident. And yes, you'd find an *x* for the day that Wynter passed away. Her death was a horrible thing, but it was also her grad-uation into eternity. God's goodness could be seen in her life, and also in her death.

Yes, God is *that* good. He redeems our tragedy and failure, and His promises are beyond our imagination. Sometimes, I temporarily lose sight of that goodness, but ultimately, I always return to my rock-solid belief that, whatever happens, God is good. Yes, He is *that good*.

Never forget to mark the spot.

15

THE THREE HARDEST DAYS

During all the years of my marriage to Wynter, I never really gave a second thought to what would happen if one of us died. That just seemed so far away, something that wouldn't happen to us for a long time. If I did think about it, I always assumed that if anyone died, it would be me. I never expended a millisecond of energy thinking about her funeral arrangements.

Then, suddenly and totally unexpectedly, it fell to me to arrange the funeral of the woman I loved. As I look back now, I see there were two primary concerns running through my head as I thought about planning the memorial for Wynter.

First, I wanted to honor her in the most meaningful way I could. I cared for her more than I have ever cared for anything or anybody in my life. When she was gone, I realized that my love was deeper and more profound than I'd even fully realized. Because of this, it was absolutely critical for me to work with the funeral home and our church to create the perfect celebration of her passing into the presence of Jesus. I wanted everything to be just right and for it to give her the highest honor. Every detail was significant to me—not only the program for the actual service, but also what she wore: her outfit and her jewelry. All of it was immensely important to me. I was surprised that I was able to focus on all the details.

Second, I realized that the planning of the funeral brought out one of my worst traits—that of being a people pleaser. All my life I've had to fight the tendency to keep everybody happy as best as I could, even when that really wasn't the best for me. I started obsessing over everyone's schedules so that no one who mattered would not be able to attend. I worried about inconveniencing this aunt or upsetting that cousin. It didn't help that some of them weren't shy about letting me know which dates worked best for them. I was so grateful that Anthony Evans pulled me aside (no more than 24 hours after Wynter's passing) and spoke these words: "Don't worry about anyone else except you and your girls, and what Wynter would have wanted. Everyone else can adjust. You just worry about the women that are yours to care for. Make every single decision for them."

This was just the advice that I needed, and that anyone needs who is facing a similar situation. I felt a burden lifted off my shoulders as I committed myself to celebrating the greatest gift God had given me in the way she would have chosen. There were only three full days between Wynter's passing and our celebration of her life. These were, without question, the three longest and most difficult days of my life. I couldn't sleep. I didn't want to eat. My mind was filled with questions of "why?" and "what if?" All I could do was lean hard on God, to fully depend upon Him, trusting that He would be my strength and sight. In my utter weakness I found His strength carrying me through. God was there for me in a way that was as real and inarguable as it has ever been.

During those three hardest of days, I also experienced moments of light. As I recounted in my mind the blessings that had come through my love for Wynter, I knew I had been given something beyond anything I'd ever dreamed. She was my best friend, my spouse, my lover, the mother of my children. And she was also a partner with me in our ongoing task of letting God's Kingdom be manifest through our imperfectly perfect union. I was both grief-stricken and grateful as I thought about our 15 wonderful years together.

I had to trust that the sovereign God, who had brought us together would be with me and lead me in the days after my Wynter season. God hadn't made a mistake. She hadn't slipped away while He was distracted. It was all part of His big plan. I didn't then, and I may never understand why this happened. But I could be confident that He did. All our days, Scripture teaches, are marked out and numbered—hers and mine. I had to rest in that. "And which of you by being anxious can add a single hour to his span of life?" (Matthew 6:27 ESV).

Holding on to that eternal perspective is what got me through. It wasn't easy, but God kept sending me what I needed to keep me on the path of trust.

16

SAYING GOODBYE AND MOVING ON

The day before Wynter's funeral, there were a lot of us crowded into my brother-in-law's house. While I spent time with my girls, everyone else took care of the essentials—cooking, cleaning, fixing their hair, laundry, and whatever else needed doing. And when I needed a break, there were lots of cousins available to find things to provide distraction. It was especially my youngest ones, who didn't know how to process what had happened, that really needed something to keep their minds off the loss.

It was typical July weather in Texas, which means hot. Staggeringly, overpoweringly hot. With all the conversation, voices, visitors, and the noise of gathered family, I realized that I just needed to get away from it all for a few minutes. I was grateful for everything everyone was doing, but honestly, I just needed a few minutes for myself. I'd hit a wall, and the grief and despair were threatening to overwhelm me.

To escape, I walked out the front door to give myself some space. I immediately was blasted by the steamy heat, which rose to meet me on the porch. I didn't care. In fact, it felt normal, and I hadn't felt normalcy for several days. I welcomed the sweat that formed on my body as I slipped on my wireless earphones and hit Play on the Spotify playlist that was already open on my phone. I needed to hear a melody or chorus that would help me find a little peace in that moment, something to calm the quiet storm that was going on in my heart.

But I didn't hear what I expected. It wasn't a song that popped up, but a motivational message from Stephen Furtick, a pastor of Elevation Church in North Carolina. I realized all at once that this was the same playlist I'd been listening to during my run the morning Wynter died. Furtick had put together a message which he delivered over a bed of music, so it was more of a motivational talk than an actual song. It had a kind of militaristic beat, and his voice had an insistent cadence. It caught my attention immediately.

Furtick's words, which were speaking directly into my ear, started soft and gentle, but began to build. He paraphrased the story found in Genesis 35. The main character of that chapter is Jacob, who was the grandson of Abraham. Abraham wasn't a perfect guy by any means—it's all right there in Genesis—but he was a man who trusted God. And out of that relationship of trust, God made three specific promises to Abraham.

First, God told him in Genesis 12 that He would bless him and make from him a great nation. God would, indeed, bless all of humanity through Abraham. In response, Abraham was willing to follow God's direction, which started with leaving his homeland. The Bible tells us that God called him to go, and the very next words are "so Abraham left." Talk about faith!

Second, while he was following God's direction, God made a promise in Genesis 15 that He was going to give him land. God described that land as big enough to contain a nation, which probably seemed over the top to Abraham, who didn't even have a nation yet. In fact, he didn't even have any children yet. It was just him and his wife, Sarah, who was barren. What made this promise even more unbelievable was that the very land whose borders God spelled out had current occupants; it was inhabited by different tribes and families who wouldn't be too impressed by Abraham's promise. Yes, inconceivable.

Third, in Genesis 18, God promised a child to Abraham and Sarah. When Sarah heard of the promise, she broke out in laughter because she was well beyond her prime childbearing years. What seemed impossible was fulfilled when Sarah gave birth to a son named Isaac, which set all the other promises in motion.

But these promises were not fulfilled overnight. There were lots of twists and turns and failures of faith along the way, but God was working. Their son, Isaac, had two sons, Jacob and Esau. The whole family was aware of the destiny that God had laid upon them and their descendants. Jacob wasn't a perfect guy, but it was him whom God chose to carry on the expectation of the great nation that would come from Father Abraham. Jacob deceived his brother and his father to obtain the blessing he wanted for himself, but because God is a God of grace, despite Jacob's failings, he carried on the line of blessing. He married Leah and Rachel after being deceived by their father, Laban, into marrying them both. It was Rachel he loved, but he ended up with two wives. The 12 sons of these two wives would become the founders of the 12 tribes of Israel. So, the blessing would be passed along, and the promises would all begin to take shape. There had been so much dysfunction in this family history, but God continued to keep His promise. It was His grace and lovingkindness, not their unwavering obedience, that kept the promise and the plan moving forward.

After a pretty poor start, Jacob seemed to get his act together as he aged. Things were trending upwards. Then, unexpectedly, his beloved Rachel died in childbirth. The Bible goes out of the way to make clear that Jacob had adored her, and now she was gone.

Before they reached their destination together, Rachel had died. How could it be that she wouldn't be able to partake of the fruits of the promise God had made? I could relate.

The Bible makes a point of mentioning this loss in passing, then it just moves on:

> As she was having great difficulty in childbirth, the midwife said to her, "Don't despair, for you have another son." As she breathed her last—for she was dying—she named her son Ben-Oni. But his father named him Benjamin (Genesis 35:17-18).

And that's where Steven Furtick's message picks up. Because I knew the backstory, its words spoke to me even more powerfully. God used these words to send a much-needed surge of confidence into my soul. Like Jacob, I had lost my wife with no warning. And I mourned over the promises I'd hoped that we would experience together, but now we would not. These are the words I heard Furtick speak:

> *So, Jacob, verse 20, is over her tomb.*
> *The dead thing.*
> *He set up a pillar.*
> *He didn't deny the pain of the loss.*
> *Jacob set up a pillar and to this day that pillar marks*
>   *Rachel's tomb.*
> *He will never be the same again.*
> *Cause it says in verse 20 that, Jacob buried Rachel.*
> *But it says in verse 21, Israel moved on.*

He goes on to say…

> *That's the new you.*
> *Come on, that's the part of you that abuse couldn't destroy,*
> *That neglect couldn't negate,*
> *That hard times couldn't break,*
> *That people couldn't steal,*
> *That the devil couldn't take away,*
> *That trouble couldn't change.*
> *It said, "Israel moved on"!*
> *He moved on!*
> *It's time for you, Israel, for you, child of God, to move on!*
> *Move on!*
> *Move on!*
> *Move on, Israel!*
> *Come on, you gotta get Simeon and Reuben*
>   *and Leah and the rest*
> *And Benjamin and Joseph*
> *And stop focusing on what you lost*
> *And move on with what you got left.*
> *Is anyone in this church moving on today?!*[3]

I must have listened to this track a dozen times that day, and at least a hundred more times over the next few months. It was exactly what I needed to hear.

It's time for you, Israel, for you, child of God, to move on!

Each time I heard Steven say this line, I felt the Holy Spirit prompting me to take on the confidence to keep pressing forward despite my abrupt and untimely loss. I felt some guilt about the idea of "moving on," as though I was somehow abandoning our dreams, but at a deeper level, I knew it was right; it resonated in my soul.

What did "moving on" mean to me? It certainly didn't mean forgetting Wynter. It meant not giving up on the Kingdom dreams that we shared. It meant going forward in my life while holding on to all the gifts that she had given to me during our years together. Like Jacob, I needed to set up a memorial to Wynter before I moved on—a memorial that consisted not only of mourning, but of honor and celebration for the person she was and what she meant to me. Jacob moved forward, but he did so by embracing Rachel's impact on his life, never forgetting the blessing of her love and the trust in God's promises that they shared. Before he moved on, he set up a pillar to memorialize the woman he had loved so dearly.

Though the Bible dispenses with the passing of Rachel in a single verse, I am 100 percent certain that there continued to be, for a time, a sizeable emotional and psychological struggle for Jacob. But he trusted God, he set up a memorial, and he kept moving forward. I knew that was exactly what I needed to do, while at the same time treasuring every memory and every reminder of Wynter's life, valuing the impact she had on my life and on those of Alena, Kaitlyn, Camryn, and Olivia... as well as all the nameless girls who had been touched by *For Girls Like You*, and all her family and friends.

That unexpected voice on my playlist had been just what I needed in order to assess where I was...and where I needed to go. I'm thankful that a few months later I was able to talk with Steven Furtick by phone and personally thank him for the message that so clarified my life at this difficult juncture.

With all my pain, I knew I needed to keep moving on. And I knew that this is exactly what Wynter would have wanted. Moving on meant moving forward while holding on to all things that were eternal. Our love, our family, our ministry, and anything else that God would allow to remain eternally and in history because of what we had together and in God.

17

LEGACY

My 12 years working with Dr. Tony Evans transformed me.

We had traveled together extensively, some years on an almost weekly basis. I stood alongside him as he spoke at churches, conferences, radio station events, and to representatives of other ministry organizations. Everywhere I went, I saw the esteem in which he was held, and as one who worked intimately with him, I can say that the adulation was well earned. He is a man of profound biblical insight, intimate relationship with God, unwavering integrity, and great humility. Besides my professional connection with him, there was also the family connection through Wynter. We often spent Sundays and holidays together, and occasionally even vacationed together.

I suppose I've heard him give hundreds of different talks, both on the road and in the church he pastors. There is, however, one talk that has been especially important to me, and it served as a boost of encouragement during my darkest days.

The talk came from a verse in the book of Acts where the Old Testament King David was used as an illustration: "Now when David had served God's purpose in his own generation, he fell asleep; he was buried with his ancestors and his body decayed" (Acts 13:36). Dr. Evans would pause, explain that life is like a board game, much like Monopoly, and that the game has only one purpose: winning. That is why we play. And our lives also have one purpose: serving God and winning for His Kingdom. The degree to which we serve His purpose will be the degree to which we have played the game well. Finally, with a serious tone, he would make this statement, which, he said, is true of Monopoly and true of the game of life: "One day they are going to close the box."

I always shuddered a little at that thought. It seemed so negative. I'd often chuckle.

But, on reflection, it is so true.

David was one of the rock stars of the Bible. He was the youngest and smallest of all his brothers, and not esteemed for his talents. That's why they put him in charge of the sheep. When Samuel was trying to choose the next king of Israel, David wasn't even in the running. But God had His own plans.

David's life was a series of triumphs and failures, of ups and downs. He made some terrible decisions and sometimes found himself caught in a web of sin. It is not the story of a perfect man of God, yet God called him a man after His own heart.

God had a plan.

David killed Goliath when everyone else was too afraid to challenge him.

He started as a shepherd and became king over all Israel.

He wrote most of the book of Psalms, a book of worship and intimacy with God.

Before they closed the box, and despite his missteps along the way, David was a victor. He fulfilled God's purposes for his life, and he left a legacy. He would be remembered as the greatest king in the history of his nation, and he would be a forefather in the genealogy of Jesus Christ. Through David, as promised, would come the Messiah, the Savior of the world. At the time, I doubt that David could ever have imagined the power of his own legacy.

No matter our imperfections, when our heart is turned toward the Lord, He can use us to fulfill our calling. Our legacy is not based upon a perfect track record, but on our submission to God's plan for our lives. It's often impossible to tell whether we are winning or losing in the game of life while we are "playing the game." Our success or failure can best be seen in retrospect, in the rearview mirror.

When the box was closed on Wynter's life, it was only then that I could fully understand her legacy, all the amazing things God had accomplished though her for the Kingdom of God.

I loved this woman with my whole heart, but I can assure you that she wasn't perfect. Just like David, she had her faults and flaws. She had her quirks, her besetting sins, and her failures. But also, like David, she was wholly committed to God and to her calling. She was, to paraphrase the Scripture verse, "a girl after God's own heart." As I lived side by side with her, I saw how her heart for God grew day by day, month by month, and year by year. She was constantly drawing ever closer to Jesus, learning to die to herself, and learning to be completely submitted to His will. People who knew her could see what was happening, and none of them were surprised at her growing influence across the country and even around the globe.

She didn't have a promising start. Her father was a drug addict who was physically, emotionally, and spiritually unavailable for his kids. So she was raised by a single mom in a poverty-stricken neighborhood in inner-city Baltimore—the kind of place where you aren't really safe until you learn the ropes and how to navigate it with great caution. At the time, Baltimore was one of the most dangerous and drug-infested cities in America, and dealers in all sorts of drugs did their business catty-corner to her home. If you looked at her from the perspective of statistical probabilities, you wouldn't have given her a chance of making anything of her life.

But God authored a different story for Wynter. He lifted her out of these circumstances and dropped her in one of the best private schools in Maryland, even though it was a school she could never even hope to afford to attend. The godly influences and financial sacrifices of grandparents and mentors and aunts and uncles made a real difference in her upbringing and in her rise out of what most would consider impoverishment. She did well in school and graduated. And along the way, she met a handsome guy, a real Prince Charming.

Well, she met me…

Her story included giving birth to our oldest daughter, Alena, who wouldn't have been brought to term if a blood clot passing through Wynter's eye during her pregnancy hadn't alerted doctors to a larger problem—a clotting disorder that typically kills the baby while still in utero. But the doctors knew in time to do something about it.

Her story included moving with me from New Jersey to Texas to launch a new life, and this opened up the time and space for her to begin to realize her dream of helping young girls.

Her story included giving birth to three more girls with no complications, despite her blood-clotting disorder. And she would also see them each receive their second birth, as each of them accepted Jesus Christ as their Lord and Savior. I had the privilege of baptizing all four of them in turn.

Her story included fulfilling her vision of helping girls by creating *For Girls Like You* magazine. God gave her exactly what she needed to accomplish this: desire, capacity, strength, and faith. It continues to grow and now has more than four times the number of subscribers it had when Wynter died. She would then publish her first book, a devotional for tweens which took the same name as the magazine, *For Girls Like You*. It was the first of eight books she wrote with Harvest House Publishers, and the last was *I Am Yours*, a book of devotions and prayers that spoke God's truth and identity into girls. Each section starts with "I Am…" and shares a truth about the girl she found herself to be in God and wanted to share with God's girls everywhere. It starts beautifully with "I Am Yours" and ends marvelously with "I Am a Bold and Beautiful World Changer."

Wynter's story included all the gratitude she felt in the accomplishments and, even more, in the character of her daughters. Alena, the oldest, acted in the film *War Room* before she was even 14 years old. She also wrote (with a little help from Wynter) a fiction series for girls called *Lena in the Spotlight*. Each one of our girls began participating in her ministry in different ways. With each passing year, Wynter saw in her girls the same confidence in Christ that she had. That was all she needed to see. Wynter was so proud of these accomplishments, but she was more concerned about her daughters being full-time Christians than in having them involved in full-time ministry. After Wynter's death, Alena's younger sisters soon followed in her footsteps and created their own stories with the Daniels' Sisters series, which is a three-book fictional series that continues their big sister's books. They are a fictional telling of our family's story.

As for Dad, well, I couldn't be more pleased with the women they are becoming. Their pain and their experience, mixed with God's grace, is forging them into women after God's own heart, just like their mother.

Wynter was an ordinary girl in every way, but God used her for some extraordinary things. I'll probably never know the full measure of the lives she impacted.

In the days after she died, I thought a lot about what kind of legacy that Wynter had left behind after her all-too-brief life. I'm grateful I could stand on the sidelines and cheer her on, and at other times work closely side by side. What she accomplished has made a major difference in the lives of countless young ladies.

Why did she have to leave so soon? I sometimes wrestle with that question, and I'm not sure that I will ever really understand. I would have loved another 15 years—maybe another 50. I would have loved for her to be able to see the girls grow into young women and then someday marry. I would have loved for us to be grandparents together, spoiling our grandchildren like all good grandpas and grandmas do.

I know that Wynter completely trusted God with her life, and I know that I have to trust Him with her life too.

Simply put, Wynter served the purposes of God for her generation, and then she fell asleep. When she woke up, she was in the arms of her Savior. And I'm confident she isn't asking the kinds of questions I was left with.

Wynter made a Kingdom investment with the life she was given. It has reaped a bountiful return. This is the same opportunity you and I have. What will we do with the opportunities He has given? What kind of return will we see on the investments we are making from day to day? It all depends on how you and I invest our lives. Wynter taught me the importance of that both in her life and in her death.

After the death of their brother, Lazarus, Jesus offered this promise to Mary and Martha: "I am the resurrection and the life. The one who believes in me will live, even though they die; and whoever lives by believing in me will never die. Do you believe this?" (John 11:25-26).

Looking back at life with Wynter and life after my Wynter season, I now see these verses in a different way. In one sense, I know Jesus is talking about eternal life and the fact that we have a life beyond this one. But I also now have this keen sense that Jesus is also talking about the reality that those who live with their lives poured out for the Kingdom of God will have a life that exists into perpetuity on this earth, even after they leave it.

Wynter has that. Her works continue to praise her and bring glory to God. The same can be true for you and me. I love how Jesus leaves it: "Do you believe this?"

—⊶⊷—

Perhaps you might want to think about your own legacy. What will you be leaving behind when you leave this earth? You might wonder how you can make that kind of difference when you don't have control over all the circumstances of your life.

For me, thinking about my own legacy is kind of an overwhelming thought. And when I say legacy, I mean the things that I'm investing in now that will matter for all eternity. I would have never expected to lose Wynter at such a young age, and there are numerous lesser unexpected detours my life has taken along the way.

It all starts, I think, by just saying yes to all that is required of you. I can look back over Wynter's life and see some of the patterns emerge, but I can assure you that she wasn't really focused on leaving a legacy as she lived her life. No, she just tried to make the right next decisions day after day. And to do a little dreaming in league with God.

It was early in our marriage when Wynter told me, "I want to write a book." Her tone was nonchalant. There wasn't any real urgency to her voice, so I didn't really take it that seriously. But when I looked at her, she had a kind of serious look on her face.

So, I asked the most logical question: "Write a book about what?"
She just said in the same sort of casual tone, "I don't know."

I forced a smile, but I was a little annoyed at her response. "Well," I said, "you may want to figure that out."

Truth is, I believed her as much as I would have if she had announced that she was planning a trip to the moon. You have to understand, I am someone who always believes in having a plan, and that if you really want to make something happen, you must have a plan. Well, Wynter clearly had no plan. I mean zero. She didn't have a topic, an idea, or even a thought about what the "book" would be about.

For the next eight years, the topic never came up again.

Meanwhile, she graduated with her degree in communications, which ironically, she specifically chose because it didn't require writing an essay to get admitted to the program. Then she became a grant writer for a short time, though she really didn't take to the technical writing. She liked to be creative. And then she worked as a ministry coordinator for a church outreach organization, but this still didn't seem like it was in her sweet spot.

Once we had the kids, she decided to focus on being a mom for nearly five years. No career. No job. That's when the idea of the magazine came along, though she didn't even call it a magazine at first. It was just a resource. She felt, finally, like she had found something that fit her gifts and her passion. Before long, it was more than just a magazine. It was a ministry brand for outreach to tween girls.

That's when Heather, one of my workmates, learned about what Wynter was doing and became convinced there could be more than just a magazine in the developing brand. Heather was a writer herself, so she introduced Wynter to a publisher she had been working with: Harvest House. Heather had caught the vision for what Wynter was doing and thought it needed more exposure. I've seen that Heather just has a strong intuition. She seems able to see beyond the things that can be seen.

I have to be honest. In those early days, I didn't really fully understand the potential of what Wynter was doing or fully appreciate her gifts. After all, it wasn't really bringing in any money, and we could always use a little extra cash. When I pressed her a bit to use her talents for something more lucrative, I always got a firm no. She knew she had a calling from God on her heart, and even then, she was beginning to make space and margin to keep saying yes to the vision He had placed in her heart.

She had always wanted to write a book. This was a desire God had placed in her heart even as a child. That seed developed over the years until the time was right—when God dropped an opportunity in her lap. The publisher asked for a book proposal. When they saw it, they turned it down. She was heartbroken. But then they asked her, "Instead, would you consider creating a devotional for girls that has the feel of your magazine?" They recognized how well she communicated to that audience and thought she could do a great job.

She said yes and set to work. The rest is history. Eight books in a short number of years. Her yes was all that was required to set everything in motion.

First the years of preparation, and then the years of the ministry that arose out of that. But the preparation was necessary for her success.

—⧓⧒—

I've had to say, "Yes, Lord" in the face of my loss. I've had to let her go and continue to trust God through all the twists and turns and unexpected circumstances. In many ways, looking back, I see that her whole life was one big yes to the God she loved.

It reminds me that God has a plan and that God has a bigger perspective than mine. Why try to make my own plans come about when I can trust Him to guide me? Proverbs 16:9 says, "In their hearts humans plan their course, but the LORD establishes their steps." And when we delight in Him, He will give us the desires of our hearts. Sometimes those desires aren't immediately obvious to us, but He is the One who will establish our steps and order them for His purposes. He always has our best in mind.

This is the hardest yes I've ever had to give. Grieving the loss of Wynter while leading my girls and working in full-time ministry has been harder, longer, and more deeply exhausting than I would ever have thought possible. But on the other side of that yes, I immediately began to sense that God was in control. He gave me a sense of gratitude that wouldn't be present if I would have chosen to say no, or to skip the pain by burying myself in distractions or things that weren't part of my yes. Even though I'm still somewhere on the journey, I can already tell you that I'm glad I said yes, and that I continue to live that out.

18

BE STILL

Earlier I shared about the two words that hang over my bed in my home in Tennessee. Each of the words is in its own frame, one large, neatly lettered word against a matte white surface on each of them: *Be Still*.

The two plaques had once been a reminder hanging over the bed I shared with Wynter, and so now they were a daily reminder. Taken from Psalm 46, in the context of trusting God in the midst of great difficulty and a present trouble, the psalmist urges us to retreat into the hands of our deliverer rather than trying to deliver ourselves. Our first thought in a trying time is to do whatever we need to do to make things better, to fight against our challenges. Instead, our first response should be to place ourselves in His hands and let Him be the One that fights the battle.

Wynter believed this, and she lived her life by this commitment. She embodied the "be still" message in her whole approach to life. When life got hard, and it definitely did sometimes, she would often retreat to the bedroom for prayer. And when she lay down for sleep every night, she would rest in the calm and peace of being still before the God she loved.

When it came time to celebrate her life, this was a common theme of many of the stories people shared about her and her life. Most spoke of a woman who knew that the best way to go to battle against your trials was to take them to the Lord and trust in Him as your deliverer.

The general expectation is that a funeral will be sad and somber, filled with heaviness and hopelessness. Wynter's was not like that at all. Though we all missed her, we rejoiced in her life—a life well lived. And we rejoiced that God had made His Word come to life through the way she lived.

Nearly a thousand people crowded into the church that day to say goodbye to a woman who had been a special friend to each of them. Many of them are names that you'd recognize if I told you, who had taken time out of their busy schedules to be there. But they were here to celebrate her, just like everyone else.

I imagined as I sat there listening to the stories that she was probably smiling down from heaven, realizing as never before how very deeply loved she was by so many different people.

Wynter sometimes struggled, as so many of us do, with wondering whether her life really mattered. Even as her ministry expanded and grew, she still wrestled with her significance. It was the lie that attempted to steal her joy in the face of many accomplishments. Even with her hands firmly grasping the plow and moving forward, I think maybe she didn't look down often enough to see how much of the soil was being turned over for the Kingdom. I think most of us wrestle with the same question about our lives, even as we try to live for God. We can't quite trust that His grace is big enough to answer that question of our meaning and purpose because from our perspective we aren't really seeing the results of what He is doing through us. If we could look from God's perspective, we would likely be amazed—just as Wynter would have been on the day of the funeral. Quietly and steadily, God is using the lives of those who surrender to His plan for them. I would never have thought I'd call a funeral epic, but Wynter's funeral was *epic*. It was beautiful, and it was a bird's-eye view of what God thought about one of His chosen servants.

As our family gathered for a viewing of Wynter's body, it became even more clear to me that Wynter was gone, that she was now in the arms of Jesus. Her body lay there in the coffin, lifeless and unmoving, and I found these words escaping from my mouth: "That's not actually her." Sure enough, it was her body in that casket, but that which made her the essential Wynter we all loved was no longer present. Just the shell that had contained her soul and spirit. It was an emotional and rather surreal time, to say the least. I felt like I was inside a movie. Time seemed to stand still, and everything normal about our lives became incredibly abnormal. I found myself experiencing peace, even as it felt like I was having some sort of out-of-body experience.

Following the private family viewing, the girls all moved backstage, except for one. Kaitlyn stayed there by my side as friends and family paraded past the coffin. I didn't want to miss the chance to acknowledge everyone's presence and thank them for being there. There I stood, about 20 feet from Wynter's body, and greeted each person with a hug or a handshake as they came forward to give their last goodbye to my wife. Kaitlyn saw what I was doing and mimicked my actions, so everyone got greeted and hugged twice. It was a powerful reminder that my children were always watching, and my actions would guide them in how they handled this difficult day. I could see in her eyes that she wanted to support me and that she didn't want to miss a moment of what God had for her that day. I know I will never forget it.

I learned early in my child-rearing days that my girls were always watching. That they were always keeping an eye on us, and were taking their cues from our actions, good or bad. It is a great responsibility. I'm reminded of the words I heard Curt Thompson, a Christian psychologist, speak at a small gathering of leaders. They so convicted me that I wrote them down: "To the degree that a parent makes sense of their own story will be to the degree that a child can be secure in theirs."

In his book *The Anatomy of the Soul*, Thompson expands on this idea: "Of all the variables that encourage the development of secure attachment in a child, the single most powerful one is the degree to which the child's parent has made coherent sense of his or her own story."[4]

Believing that this is true, I am so grateful for my faith, and the way that it has helped me to make sense of my own story, to see the purposes in all the twists and turns my life has taken. And I can see how it has influenced my girls as well, helping them to deal with the unexpected tragedy that goes beyond our ability to really understand. I've learned that some of the most crucial events in our spiritual journey just don't have easy explanations or can't be fully understood. Faith is trust. It's believing even when you cannot see.

It is being still.

⚊⚊

Wynter would have loved the memorial service in her honor. And in some way, I think she was probably smiling down upon it as we celebrated a life well lived.

It started with a song from Anthony Evans, Wynter's favorite singer. I'd worked with him to create a list of songs that I knew Wynter loved. And, no surprise to anyone who knew Wynter, each of them was a worship song. Each of them spoke of trusting God in whatever circumstances we might find ourselves. After all my years managing Anthony's music career, it was great to get back together to create one more glorious concert. As he lifted his voice and led, the entire crowd joined in. And one of the songs that the whole congregation sang was the one I had whispered into Wynter's ear as she lay dying.

And then came the time for some key people to share about Wynter and her life.

Through tears and smiles, Chrystal Evans described Wynter as a woman who worked from a place of rest. She jokingly told all those in attendance that she never knew anyone who watched as many movies and shows on Netflix or took as many naps as Wynter did. And yet, Wynter accomplished so much in her short life. She believed that this was because Wynter was a yes girl, but she only said yes to the things she knew God was calling her to. Everything else was an easy no because if God wasn't leading her, then it wasn't hers to do! She would operate from that "be still" place, trusting God to do the heavy lifting on most of life, until He gave her a specific task to achieve. Then she worked diligently and swiftly, and with great concentration. Everything else could wait, but God's commands could not.

As I listened to Chrystal, I was convicted because I am not like Wynter in that way. I tend to be a people pleaser, always looking for how I can keep everybody happy. For me, saying no is always a battle, though I had made some progress through living all those years with a yes girl. She'd even helped me gather the courage to turn down the opportunities that arose which I really didn't need to pursue. It felt hard to decline, but often later I would see the wisdom in saying no. I am still learning the lesson of "be still."

"Be still" comes from Psalm 46, a psalm of three symmetrical stanzas meant to be sung between the congregation of Israel and their spiritual leaders, the Levites. The phrase comes near the end of this song of victory, a reminder of the triumph that was theirs in being part of God's Kingdom and God's plan. It is the same kind of reminder for Christians today.

You might want to look up and read the whole psalm, which speaks of God's control in whatever trouble, uproar, or struggle you might be facing. Because He is in control, we don't have to be. We can be still. Even when, as in verse 2, it seems like the world is collapsing all around us and the mountains are falling "into the heart of the sea." Even during such upheaval, we can trust Him. In verse 6, the psalmist describes the turmoil of nations rising against each other. Even then, he says, we can trust and be still. God is there with us in the midst of every calamity and in all the chaos that swirls around us. He is waiting to show us His strength, His power, His plan, and ultimately, His victory.

He doesn't say that He will keep us from experiencing all these hard things, but He says He will be with us in the midst of them.

I felt the truth of this psalm in the darkest days following Wynter's death. In fact, I don't know that God's presence was ever more real to me than then, when I needed Him most. I wasn't happy. I felt the darkness crowding in around me. I was shaken to my very core. But through all this, I knew I could be confident that He was with me and that I was never alone.

Not only was He there for me, but I saw in powerful ways how He was there for my girls.

When Scott Wilson, the man whom we would come to call our pastor, took the stage at the funeral, he made a special point of reaching out to my daughters. Scott had been our pastor for about seven years, and he had also become our friend and confidant. He had walked me through the difficult decision about taking the new job in Tennessee. I am a loyal person at heart, so I was struggling with my loyalty to Dr. Evans and the ministry. After all, he was more than my boss. He was my spiritual father. He was my hero. The very thought of disappointing him made me sick to my stomach. But I knew, at the deepest level of my being, that this was God's leading. When he saw how I was struggling, Scott pulled me aside and said, "What's right for Jonathan Pitts is right for Wynter Pitts, is right for Tony Evans, is right for Church of the City (which had called me), is right for the Evans family, and is right for everyone that is walking in God's ways." He was, in other words, reminding me of the truth of Romans 8:28. And so, he helped me to walk in obedience to this new calling in my life.

Scott walked over and bent down in front of my little girls, who were sitting in the front row. He wasn't worried about wrinkling his nice suit or about delaying the service. His full focus was on my daughters' hearts and you could see this in his eyes. One of the team members had placed a small pile of Wynter's books on a small table, and he picked them up, one by one, as he used their titles to remind them of their mommy's love and care for them. His voice cracked a little, overcome with emotion and compassion. He shared that for every author, their books are the message of their life.

And then he asked them a question: "If your mommy's books are the message of her life, I wonder what Wynter would say to her girls right now?"

Picking up one of her devotionals, *You're God's Girl*, he uttered its title in his words of encouragement: "She would tell you, you're God's girls. So, don't be listening to the voices of this world. You go to the One who made you because you're His girl."

Next, he reminded them of how much Wynter and I loved them. He wanted them to know that this was the truth beyond a shadow of a doubt. It was what was in her heart when she wrote *She Is Yours*. "Do you know what your parents told God?" he asked, holding up that book, "She is yours. They were fixated on you, and they loved you, but they knew that they couldn't control you. They said, 'God, she is yours' in respect to each of you."

Then he held up Wynter's latest book—one that had only been released 14 days prior to her passing: *God's Girl Says Yes*. His voice dropped to a whisper. The words that came next could be heard by the whole crowd, but they were clearly intended especially for my daughters: "You know what God's girls do? They say yes. God has this incredible plan for your life. He's put passions and skills and talents inside you. Each of you was made with a purpose. You unlock God's greatness for you when you say yes. And that's the very essence of your mom's life."

There wasn't a dry eye in that room, over which a silence had descended.

Finally, he uttered his final words to the girls, using the title of what would be the last book she would publish (which wouldn't come out for almost another year—a book of prayers entitled *I Am Yours*): "Your mom's heart is that she would say 'I am Yours' to the Lord. She lived her entire life saying, 'I am Yours.'"

It was like Wynter was, through her books, letting them know how much she loved them, and how her hope was that they would follow her path of devotion to God. At this point, Scott had four of his staff members bring beautiful gold necklaces with Wynter's birthstone to each of the girls—a tangible reminder that her words and wisdom would always accompany them through the ups and downs of their lives, a sign of their mother's love and the love of the church that would be there to support them.

I knew in that emotional moment that the God of the entire universe, the One whom I had served all of my life, whom I had trusted and followed, who knew every hair on my head, and who has all power in His hands—that One was fighting for me and my girls. I needed it. I was weary and tired and a little bit numb. I had no power to fake any emotion. I just needed Him, and He was there.

Scott had opened the service with these words: "We are people of faith. We know where Wynter is right now. Her life was a full range of living, so this home-going service should be a full range of emotion." It was.

He ended the final prayer of the service by asking God to "let Your anointing and Your peace rest in this place." And it did.

I could not help but let a little smile escape. God was reminding us that He was in control.

We just needed to be still.

19

FINISHING WELL

When the time came to lay Wynter's body to rest the next morning, we chose a beautiful wooded area in the part of Dallas where we'd raised our children. The day was sunny and bright, but our mood was somber. It wasn't easy to think about burying Wynter here in Texas and then moving the family to Tennessee. Frankly, it was a little bit surreal.

At the burial, with tears in his eyes and a tremor in his voice, my twin brother read from a devotional that he'd discovered in my sister-in-law's bathroom a few days prior to the funeral. It seemed to say what needed to be said, and it beautifully summed up Wynter's life. It was written by her "sister cousin" Priscilla Shirer, who was Wynter's favorite Bible teacher, and it spoke again to my heart, just as it had when my brother read it to me before the burial service. It's from her devotional book *Awaken: 90 Days with the God Who Speaks*, and the piece is called "Finishing Well."

Ben cleared his throat and read these words:

> Could anyone other than David have been a more natural
> choice to oversee the construction of Israel's first perma-
> nent house of worship? Imagine the disappointment, per-
> haps even the confusion he must have felt when trying to

digest the news he'd been given by the prophet Nathan that someone else would enjoy this honor instead?

David was faced with a choice: either selfishly insist on fulfilling his own ambitions, or step aside and willingly pass on the baton to the one whom God had appointed to complete the task. He chose wisely. Instead of succumbing to hubris or acceding to selfish ambition, he cleared the way for the next one in line. He didn't scramble to maintain his position or usurp the assignment God had delegated to another. He trusted. He submitted. He finished well... by *not finishing*.

I wonder how many divine missions, mandates, and ministries are aborted by self-minded Christians who refuse to relinquish control of the task to those who follow in their footsteps. I wonder how many worthy pursuits have lost their spiritual relevance and vitality because someone greedily clung to their personal ownership of it, rather than cheerfully stepping aside, encouraging its growth and maturity into a new generation.

One of the more difficult nuances of victorious Christian living is that of staying sensitive to the Spirit's timing, of knowing when He's whispering, "Enough now, My child." Only the truly humble heart will comply when it's time to let others carry the reins of responsibility forward while their own assignment shifts to another role. But just as an Olympic relay is dependent on each successful exchange of the baton, so are churches, ministries, families, and visions dependent on faithful leaders who will yield power when it's someone else's turn to carry the torch.

"Finishing well" can sometimes mean not seeing the full end of what you started, but rather stepping away so others can share in the victory of a race well run.

The fact is, the glorious building that rose from the city of David is still remembered, all these centuries later, as

"Solomon's Temple." Before its demoralizing destruction at the hand of pagan invaders centuries later, its opulence was known far and wide as being reminiscent of its builder's esteem. *Solomon's Temple.* And yet Solomon's success was largely due to David's selfless release, and also to something more—something beautiful and staggering in its generosity. According to 1 Chronicles 22, David used the remainder of his lifetime to collect the materials, delegate the workforce, fund the expenses, and enthusiastically validate his son before the entire nation. He paved the path for his replacement's success.

Not everything is yours to finish. Many tasks of great kingdom importance may not be wholly synchronized with your own lifetime or your particular generation. Still, choose to gratefully be a part of what God is doing by fully investing yourself in His greater work.

Yes, the work is *His.* And since it is, release it back to Him whenever He asks you to, trusting that the scope of it will be beyond your wildest imagination.[5]

And then, just like that, whether we were fully ready for it or not, we were forced to turn the page. Like Jacob, when he buried Rachel, and like so many people before us, our family would be forced to bury the one we loved, set up a memorial, and move on.

20

THE NEXT CHAPTER

God knows what we need long before we do.

All four of my girls were already signed up to go to a weeklong Christian camp called Pine Cove, which started the day after the burial. It was a regular yearly event, and something they always looked forward to with great anticipation. This year was different, of course, but it turned out to be exactly what they needed. Less than two hours after Wynter's burial service, we loaded up the van and, along with Wynter's cousins and their kiddos, made the hour and a half drive to east Texas to drop them off for a week of camp. At first I was pretty reticent about going ahead with what we had been planning for months, but I realized it would probably be good for me to have the time to myself and that it would provide them with the ability to decompress from the stress of the last few days. They needed a little escape from reality, but it turned out that they got more than that. The camp counselors were trained in dealing with loss and grief, and we let them know in advance what to expect from my girls. I was confident that they were in good hands. And time proved me right. The whole experience was one of healing for each of my daughters.

Honestly, I was so weary and exhausted that I couldn't think straight, and I knew I wouldn't be much good to them or anyone else. Following the funeral, I just had nothing left to give in my brain or my heart.

The girls could keep busy at camp, and I could do what I needed to do most: sleep. I hadn't slept more than an hour straight for five days, but now the darkness was lifting as the initial shock just settled into a sadness that I could cope with. So, I slept. A lot. And when I wasn't sleeping, I hung out with my family. I was mourning the best I could, which, for me, meant letting my mind do absolutely nothing. That week without the kids was a week of recovery for me, a way to decompress and try to find a new normal.

———⟆⟅———

And then it was time to embrace the next chapter in our life, which was in almost every way a different life than we'd been living before. According to our former plan, I would become the executive pastor at Church of the City in Franklin, Tennessee, we would move into our new home and unpack all our belongings, the kids would be enrolled in their new schools, and we would open up a brand-new post office box for Wynter's ministry.

Before they left for camp, the girls wanted to know if anything was going to change. Were we still going to move? It was a reasonable question, and one I was already asking myself. Would it make more sense to stay in Dallas now? After all, this is where all our family support could be found. Would it be wiser to unwind all our plans and just stay put?

The best answer I could give them is that I needed time to think, and especially, to pray. I was trying to sound wise and thoughtful, but truthfully, I didn't have a clue what I should do. All the plans were in place, but my normal aversion to risk was telling me that maybe we should just stay put, stick with the life we knew. I was pretty confident that Dr. Evans would hire me back if I wanted to stay. But, I had to ask myself, was all my earlier clarity about God's will just a mistake? Honestly, I didn't think so. But at this point, with my emotions worn and fraying, I wasn't sure I could trust myself to make a good decision. And my partner who normally talked me through such decisions was an eternity away. God would have to find a way of confirming what He wanted me to do. And He did.

Just two days before the funeral, Alena pulled me aside and asked me if we could take a walk together. "Sure," I said.

At 14, Alena possessed a wisdom far beyond her years. She is someone who thinks deeply about things and doesn't just take everything at face value. She has a very serious streak. I remembered that the last time she suggested a walk, it was because she wanted to talk about a boy she liked and that she didn't quite know how to process her feelings. During that discussion, she had told me something that made my heart sing. She told me that she wanted to have a deeper relationship with me, not like the kind that most daughters had with their dad, but something really special. It is a moment I will always treasure. That's why, when she suggested a walk, I knew that something must be up.

As we slowly shuffled along down the street, we talked for a few minutes about how much we were already missing her mommy. It was hard for both of us to completely admit to ourselves that she was gone, and we bonded over the pain we were feeling.

Then, she came to a stop, and I turned to look at her. A serious look came over her face as she decided it was time to cut to the chase: "Dad, are we still moving to Nashville?"

I fumbled a bit with how to respond. "That's a good question. I, um, think we just need to pray about it and take our time with the decision." I knew that I had some time. My new boss, Pastor Darren Whitehead, had given me permission to take my time so that I wouldn't make any rash decisions, which was really wise and really compassionate.

I was about to continue, planning to make my spiritual points about seeking God in all this, when Alena cut me off. "Daddy," she said, "Mommy was more excited about Nashville than any of us. She was excited for you and for the church. I think we are supposed to go."

Her words caught me completely off guard. I wasn't surprised by the maturity of her thinking, but I was not expecting to hear her speak with the kind of confidence she was expressing. There was no hesitancy. She had every reason to want to stay in Texas. Her friends, her family, her school, and everything that she normally depended upon were here in Dallas. I wouldn't have blamed her if she made an impassioned plea to stay put. But she didn't. I'm convinced that she knew, difficult as the move might be, that it was the right thing. It was the direction in which God was calling not just me, but our family.

"Okay," I responded. I really didn't know what to say. As soon as she said it, I felt a wave of confirmation and comfort sweep over me. It was, I think, in that split second that I decided we needed to move forward with our original plan. I normally wouldn't have let the words of a 14-year-old make the decision for me. But her voice of reason sounded exactly like what Wynter would have said.

I flashed back to the moment when I was worrying about who we were going to offend or disappoint if I accepted the job, and Wynter said simply and firmly, "Jonathan, I think this is right." Her confidence had given me strength, and now Alena's words were also confirming that we were on the right path.

<hr />

God was gracious enough to "seal the deal" on moving forward when I got a phone call from Darren. He was scheduled to begin being my new boss the following Monday, and he called me just a few hours after Alena and I had taken our walk together. His tone was caring and warm, and he said he wanted to check in and see how I was doing. Frankly, I didn't know him very well. We hadn't had much interaction other than our lengthy interview process and a couple meals with him and his wife, Brandy. But I let him know that we were doing as well as could be expected. Then, after a moment of pause, he spoke these words: "Jonathan, I just want you to know that if you decide to stay in Dallas, we will fully support you in that. We'll figure out how to get your belongings back to you and help you sell the house. We want you to make the best decision for your family."

I knew he meant it, and I wasn't surprised. It was what I would have expected from a great leader, which is what I was discovering him to be. But his next words were not what I was expecting. "But if you come," he said, "you will find a church family ready to adopt you."

In other words, he wanted to say "no pressure," but he also wanted to offer a promise. And this reminded me that God had a plan all along.

He would use my new brothers and sisters (my new family in Tennessee) as part of my healing and His provision.

I thought about our dinner together with Darren and Brandy after we had said yes to the new position. While our kids joined theirs on their trampoline, laughing and giggling with joy, we talked about our future ministry together, and Darren made a special point of saying that he was as excited about having Wynter as part of their community as he was having me as a pastoral partner. They believed in the *For Girls Like You* ministry and intended to give it their full blessing and support.

I thought about just weeks before Wynter died, when we had joined Dr. Evans and the rest of the Evans clan for a fabulous two-day Fourth of July holiday trip to the lake. They had prayed over us and our new ventures, and my sister-in-law, Andrea, had created a lovely picture book of memories with our families over the past 14 years, as well as a book of hand-written notes that gave everyone a chance to express what we meant to them and how much they would miss us when we moved to Tennessee. In retrospect, it gave them an opportunity to say how much they loved Wynter and me, and I'm glad she got to read these words before she died. They didn't realize they were saying a more permanent goodbye to her than what they'd planned.

My mind snapped back. I sat there on this phone call, trying to fully process what Darren was saying. I'm someone who has always been focused on giving, on accomplishing something, on helping out as much as I can. I wasn't used to being on the receiving end. My whole career had been based around serving others in their ministries. But what I could do for them wasn't Darren's focus, nor would he be naïve enough to think I could do anything much right now. The phrase that stood out to me were these words: "You will find a church family ready to adopt you." That moved me more than I can say.

And then he let me know that if we were coming, he had been promised two more spots for our youngest two daughters at Grace Christian Academy, which we had looked at during our visit. We immediately knew that this wonderful and Christ-centered school would be perfect for the girls, but were disappointed to learn that though they had space for our two oldest, there was no availability for our two youngest. The fourth grade was completely booked up and had no room for more students. Wynter had been pleading with the Lord to open up two spots in the fourth grade for our twins just a week earlier. Honestly, I wasn't praying, because I didn't see how we could afford to send all four daughters there anyway. While she prayed, I counted my blessings, not asking God to do anything more. He had already done enough in my view.

I could now barely keep up with what Darren was saying: "Mr. Mason, the school headmaster, heard that Wynter had passed away, and they knew that you had been trying to get your two youngest daughters into the school. Their board wanted you to know that if you guys decide to come, they want to make sure that all four of your girls are welcome. They've made a way for them to be together."

I couldn't believe it. As his words began to register, I realized that God was answering the prayers that Wynter had been praying, even as she was now with Him in heaven. Her answered prayers had outlived her. This miraculous response confirmed to me that God had a plan, and that He was still working on our behalf—even for things I hadn't even bothered to pray for! We were not forgotten or overlooked. He was still moving us along the path He'd forged for our family. I smiled to think of how Wynter would have approved.

It was hard to take in all this kindness. That cynical little voice inside kept warning me that there had to be a catch: *There's no way that they are going to do all that for us. And even if they do, it will only be temporary. I won't be able to pay the tuition for all four of the girls, and we'll eventually have to pull them out. I don't want them to be disappointed.* But still, I knew I had to trust God and accept the gift being offered.

It was a struggle for me to accept such a gift. Honestly, sometimes it is still a struggle for me to receive all the good gifts God has provided through the kindness of others. I think that my orphan heart is always desperately trying to avoid being hurt or disappointed. But I am learning. God has given so much and done so much through the care of others that I am starting to get better at just accepting it and being grateful. It's still a journey for me though.

There was still one more surprise coming.

Darren also shared that the school wanted to know if our twins, our fourth graders, would want to be in the same classroom, or separate ones. Little did he or Mr. Mason know this was also a prayer in Wynter's heart. I couldn't believe it. Wynter had so much wanted them to be in class together and had met a fair resistance to the idea from the public school we had enrolled them in after learning there was no room in the private school. But in typical Wynter style, she wouldn't take no for an answer. She pleaded with the administrator, and she pleaded with the Lord. And now, exactly what she had wanted would come to pass, but in the school she had been praying about as well. Two prayers. Two answers. Both yes. In terms of the girls' education, God had met every desire of Wynter's heart. She had been grateful for her own experience in a private school and the way it changed the trajectory of her life, and she wanted that same opportunity for her beloved girls. Now they were going to have it at a great school with a Christian perspective on education. I couldn't help but wish Wynter was there to see it all fall into place. Somehow, though, I think she knew.

As to my financial worries, well, those seemed to be misplaced. God opened the doors, and God found a way to help me pay for the tuition. God's kindness has worked itself out in so many ways and his goodness has continued to abound. My worries were misplaced, and God continues to replace them with a greater faith. It hasn't been a burden at all. I sometimes wonder if Wynter, when she got to heaven, pulled Jesus aside and said, "Jonathan's gonna stress out, so can we help him out down there?"

Now, there wasn't any question. We were on our way to Tennessee. Ready for our next chapter.

21

EXTRAVAGANT LOVE

In Paul's letter to the Ephesians, he reminds the church in that city of God's marvelous plan for their lives. He talks about God's intentions, God's power, and God's grace. And he tells them that sometimes God's way of working out His plans can be a bit mysterious and unexpected. There will be rough patches. There will be suffering and disappointment. Of all people, he knew. He had experienced many hardships and setbacks. But he was grateful for the way that God had used them in his life and ministry.

His prayer in chapter 3 reminded the Ephesian Christians that they are a family, and that they had a Father whose love was unfathomable. His words describing our relationship with God and with each other are surely among the most beautiful in all of Scripture:

> So that Christ may dwell in your hearts through faith. And I pray that you, being rooted and established in love, may have power, together with all the Lord's holy people, to grasp how wide and long and high and deep is the love of Christ (Ephesians 3:17-18).

These words capture the mysterious and awesome power of God's love, and it is important to remember that Paul wrote these at a time of personal suffering as a prisoner for the gospel of Jesus. The context makes the words especially potent. During such a hard time in his own life, he could celebrate who God was and the special relationship he had with his brothers and sisters in Christ. By implication, he seems to be saying that if he can get through such hardships by the grace of God, so can they.

And then comes this soaring proclamation of total and absolute trust—a passage I always loved but only fully understood after my experience of losing Wynter:

> Now to him who is able to do immeasurably more than all we ask or imagine, according to his power that is at work within us, to him be glory in the church and in Christ Jesus throughout all generations, for ever and ever! Amen (Ephesians 3:20-21).

The promise given here changes everything. God will not only answer our prayers, but even do more than we could ask or imagine! We can't even begin to wrap our minds around the truth and extent of God's love. It is just extravagant beyond words.

During this difficult season of my life, I have been reminded anew, again and again, of how much God loves me. I always used to think in terms of His "enoughness"—that He would always be enough for me. That I could be content with my daily bread and the meeting of my needs. I believed that He would always be enough for me. But I was worried about asking for too much—that I was being selfish if I did. And I wasn't fully convinced at the deepest level that He really was that concerned about helping me outside of the basics.

Believing that God is enough is fine from a theological standpoint, but I am learning by experience that His provision isn't all He wants to offer. Sure, He is enough, but what He wants to do in my life is more than enough. He wants to show me His extravagant love for me, immeasurably more than I can even ask for or imagine.

I don't know about you, but that frees me up to ask for more. Just like one of my little girls, not afraid to ask God for the moon! Are you willing to ask? To ask for God's absolute best for our marriages and families and ministries? To not just ask for a good enough relationship or a good enough anointing for ministry, but to ask for God's immeasurable best? These are the kinds of prayers that God was teaching me to pray, even during my darkest weeks and months. And I now offer them more consistently, more freely, and more simply than ever before because I trust that He isn't just waiting to say no for no good reason.

22

A HIGHER ALTITUDE

The God who wants to be more than just enough is the God who cares about everything that concerns us—even the seemingly small things.

During our initial preparations for our move before Wynter died, she was concerned about a detail that we hadn't figured out yet. We had a little black Yorkie Poo dog named Max. We'd left him with a dog sitter in Dallas as we were making our final preparations, but we were really concerned about the long car trip to our new home. What you need to know about Max is that he is about the most anxious dog you can imagine. Wynter knew that he wouldn't do well on a long journey in the car. I was looking for a "just enough" solution and suggested we just drug him so that he would be unconscious for most of the time. Wynter didn't like that solution at all. And she prayed for a better one.

When it finally did come time to make the move, and it would just be me and the girls, a gentleman named Bryan from our new church became our solution. Bryan was a pilot and had his own corporate jet and felt in his heart that it was his job to ease our transition. He asked Darren if he could make it easier by picking up the girls and me from a private airport near their camp. I was overwhelmed by his offer, especially given the complicated logistics that would otherwise be in play. I was also a little nervous to ask him a question that popped into my brain. Would he be open to flying Max along with us? I figured that this could be the deal breaker, but he told me that they often brought their own dog along on flights. Their plane, he said, was more like their flying minivan! That would mean only a few hours of stress for Max instead of days. So, he flew to Texas (at what I am sure was a considerable cost) and ferried our family and our little Yorkie Poo quite comfortably to our new home. Once again, Wynter's prayers had been abundantly answered even after her death. The theme continued... "immeasurably more."

Still, it was initially a somber flight. I was exhausted from the events and emotions of the previous 11 days. In one sense, it felt like those 11 days had been more like 11 years, as though the hands on the clock were moving at only a fraction of their normal speed, tediously forward ever so slowly and dragging me along with them. In another sense, the previous 11 days were a blur. So much had happened, and all so quickly. I was physically and emotionally spent.

The light jet hummed and shook, and then seemed to leave the Texas tarmac with the greatest of ease. I had taken my place in the copilot's seat next to my new friend and fellow church member, and we made small talk as we climbed up to cruising altitude. There were just enough seats in the back for the girls, and Max sat on Alena's lap. As the flight went on, and he grew more comfortable, Max hopped from seat to seat, just as though we were flying through the air in our minivan. When we reached our cruising altitude of 41,000 feet, a stillness rose all around us as we settled in for the flight. I entered into a sense of peace that I hadn't experienced in days. From this height, I could see for miles in every direction. As Bryan kept track of the instruments, we occasionally made some small talk through our headphones as he pointed out landmarks, but mostly it was quiet. Looking down at the clouds and the ground below, I had the feeling that I was leaving all the chaos of these recent days behind. And there, above the clouds, I asked God to give me a new perspective, and to let this moment of peace be the first step on a brand-new journey. At present, there high in the air, Bryan was in the "driver's seat." When we touched down, I knew that from then on I needed to let God take that place.

Whenever things had gotten a little bumpy in my life, it was always my tendency to try to grab the wheel and steer toward the direction that seemed safest. During a time of grief, it was also a temptation. But the more I tried to take control and hold on with a death grip, the more difficult things would become. I needed to trust God and take my place in the passenger seat. I needed to leave the flying to Him, just as I trusted Bryan to pilot the plane.

Through the whole experience of losing Wynter, I have experienced this truth over and over: God is an amazing pilot. He knows where He is taking me, and He will lead me in His way and in His timing if I will just settle back and let Him be in control. His heart and His voice can be relied upon, even when life throws some turbulence our way. He has a perspective where He sees things in a way I'll never see them. He's working at a much higher altitude!

⎯⎯⎯

In time, we crossed the eastern border of Arkansas into Tennessee and over Memphis as we prepared for the descent into Nashville. Once we started the approach, and the plane began to descend through the fluffy clouds, I began to worry again. What would life be like without Wynter? How would our family weather this new season? I had always leaned on Wynter for self-confidence about being a husband, a father, and a leader. Now I would be on my own. I leaned back against the seat, feeling a mixture of optimism and fear about this next phase of our journey.

But, despite my fears, I could not deny that God had been leading at every step, even as His sovereign hand ripped the most delicate and beautiful part of my life away from my grip. He had taken, but He had given, and He was continuing to give.

I trusted completely. I was completely afraid.

I was keenly aware of the paradox that I was living out.

And so, when we had landed, we stepped out of the plane and into the relative unknown.

23

NEW HOME, NEW FAMILY

We loaded everything into Bryan's car, which was already waiting there on the tarmac. We felt a little like royalty, getting special treatment. Leaving the airport, we drove through Nashville, a city I knew pretty well from having made numerous trips here with Anthony. For the girls, though, it was mostly all new, and they gazed in wonder at all the uniqueness of "Music City, USA." It took almost half an hour to get to Franklin, where our new home was located. I was feeling some nervous anticipation as we drew near. Once we got to the housing development, we made a left-hand turn into our neighborhood, and our house came into view.

There, standing on the lawn with brightly colored balloons and handmade signs of welcome, were more than a hundred people. Momentarily, I thought it might be a neighborhood barbecue, but I quickly realized that the church had turned out to welcome us to our new home and our new community. Bryan eased into the driveway, and we found ourselves surrounded by our new family—a family that we had never met. I only recognized a couple of faces. The love flowing from the gathered people was palpable. My eyes brimmed with tears that I couldn't hold back.

This was not just our new house. We were home.

There was a lot of laughing and embracing. Along with the church members, there were people who lived in the houses nearby. One of the pastors, who goes by the name CZ, and another named Jake prayed aloud for us—for peace and healing, for our current grief, and for the future that stood awaiting us. Each of us were mentioned by name. It wasn't just about me, but about my whole family. Then, a smaller group led us inside the house where there was a lovely meal waiting for us. The whole experience was like an incredible embrace of love and welcome.

If you were to visit my home today, there are still signs of that amazing first day. Each person who came brought a small stone on which they wrote a scripture, words of hope, drawings of faith, or reminders of God's love. The combined message of all these stones was that the God of all creation is with us wherever we are on our journey through life. That He loves us and cares for us and walks beside us through the darkest valleys. That there is nowhere you can go that you will not find His presence. I've kept these stones piled up on my porch, a tactile reminder of His grace and goodness—stones of remembrance. As long as I live in this house, those stones will remain—a reminder of the day God let us know that we were where we belonged.

———

The Sunday before we had arrived, Pastor Darren had climbed onto the stage and told our story to the congregation. He let them know that originally I was planning on bringing my five "ladies" with me, but that now it would only be four; that I would be coming without my wife and co-laborer in family and ministry, and my girls without their mother. As he looked out over the congregation, he cast the same vision for the church as he had for me—adopting our family. And clearly, they had taken this call seriously. They took up a generous love offering to help meet the financial needs brought on by the transition. Yet again, "immeasurably more." The things we needed, many of which we hadn't even anticipated, began to show up on at our front door.

The week we had closed on the house, Krista, our relator, had a conversation with Wynter about our kitchen table back in Texas. It was square and it wouldn't fit very well into the new kitchen. Somehow the word got around, and when we arrived, there was a lovely round table that was a perfect fit and the perfect design. Wynter would have loved it at first glance.

Then there was our bonus room over the garage, which could be reached by climbing some steps in the back of the house. I briefly pondered using it as a room for rent to help cover the cost of the mortgage, but Wynter wouldn't hear of it. She envisioned it as a beautiful guest room for friends and family, or one we could offer as temporary shelter for people in need of short-term housing. In fact, our sweet new friends Johnny and Janelle and their two daughters would need such a place shortly after we arrived. So, before I arrived with the girls, Johnny and some of the women in the church had already remodeled and furnished it, just like Wynter would have wanted. It was perfect for anyone traveling through, and we even built a small kitchenette into it a couple months later. Another generous gift. Over the years, it has proven to be the perfect place for all our friends and family who come to see us, which are many and often.

There was such an outpouring of love and care for us, and so much attention to our practical needs. It started the day we pulled into Nashville, and it continues to this day.

―⁅⁆―

There are so many people who were there for us in the days following our loss and our resettlement in Franklin, Tennessee. Their investment in our lives was a confirmation of the fact that the Lord is near to the brokenhearted.

I think of David and Judy. We'd never met them before our move to Franklin. But they spent an extraordinary amount of time over several days helping us unpack our belongings. They shuttled my daughters to practices. They made sure that there were always fresh coffee beans in the canister to provide me with the caffeine I needed to get through the mornings. And one time, when I was away traveling and it looked like Alena would be home alone, they invited her to come stay with them.

I think about Julie and John. Both of them were busy with their work in the executive office of the church, but they always found time to help us out with many of the details involved in setting up our home. They purchased some decorative knickknacks and found places for them, they touched up the paint where needed, and they hung up a lot of our pictures. They wanted to be sure that our new house felt like a home. Their gifting is insane, and my family has been a humble recipient of it over and over again.

Julie and John's mom, Diane, was also such a help. She was around so much that my daughters began calling her by her special name, Shou-che-bye, which is pronounced "sushi-bye." She came over regularly to clean and straighten things up. She would never accept a dime for the more than six months she was like a visiting maid. She did it out of joy and as a way to serve the God that she had come to love. We were just His means. Our nervous dog, Max, took a special liking to her, and she still dog sits for us from time to time.

Then there's Trina, Wynter's mother's youngest sister. Aunt Trina had a salon in the basement of her mother's house and taught Wynter all that she needed to know about washing and styling hair. Since we had four daughters, this knowledge came in very handy and saved us a lot of money over the years. One day, on our tenth anniversary, I sat down and figured out that Wynter's skills had saved us more than $27,000 in salon visits. Pretty amazing, right? Not long before Wynter's death, Trina had closed down her salon and hair business, and decided to follow her dream of traveling. She got a job as a reservation agent at an airline so that she could get free travel to go just about anywhere she wanted. One of the first things on her itinerary was to come visit her niece in Dallas. She loaded Wynter and the girls into the car for a road trip to Austin, Texas. This ended up being their farewell trip together just weeks before Wynter passed. Now, with Wynter gone, Aunt Trina decided to fly to Franklin once a month to take care of the girls' hairstyle needs. Thanks to her generosity, I've never had to worry about my daughters and their hair—which, of course, is very important to them and to me!

Another couple, Margaret and Aaron, had asked Wynter and me

to mentor them on their marital journey, which we had done over the years. Since Margaret also has styling skills, she has been willing to step in whenever Aunt Trina isn't available. And my girls always enjoy hanging out with their two boys. In a very real sense, they are family.

My list of people who have blessed our lives in countless practical ways could go on and on. There's Ken and Oksana, Dan and Danielle, Devan and Fallon. And many, many more. Of special note are all the members of the church who didn't know us before we moved, but who have become precious friends. They leveraged their lives and their resources to make sure my girls and I felt welcome. They were not just fellow church members, but family—the family we share in our faith in God.

Because of everyone's graciousness and generosity, I can say that to this day I've never wanted for anything. For a guy who used to have a lot of trouble accepting gifts, this was an overwhelming experience and a powerful lesson on how God uses us to provide for each other. God's provision for each of us usually comes through the conduit of the service of others. And His love often comes to us through a smile or act of kindness of another person. I've learned to be content with accepting all the love and kindness as a gift from God. Not something I needed to earn or deserve, but a pure gift from above. And I've learned to be that conduit. To give generously, beyond what seems reasonable. After all, God's standard is "immeasurably more."

God sends His surrogates to us in many different shapes and sizes and with a variety of different giftings. He comes to us through friends, and sometimes through strangers. God uses us all to meet one another's needs. This is an important element of what it means to live as brothers and sisters in the family of God and in the Kingdom of God.

I know that what I have gone through has given me an understanding of how to help those who are grieving from a major loss. But I also know that I need to be bold enough just to step out and be a friend to those experiencing other kinds of struggle. Watching how others had flocked to my side has been a master class in love and service.

I've had to ask myself what kind of friend I have been to others when I experience the miracle of others flocking to my side in my time of need. More than once I have said this to myself: *Lord, have I got a lot to learn about what being a friend truly looks like!* "One who has unreliable friends soon comes to ruin, but there is a friend who sticks closer than a brother" (Proverbs 18:24).

God isn't asking for our obedience because He fears that we might be enjoying ourselves and wants to put that to a stop. Definitely not. Obedience opens our eyes and opens our hearts to seeing needs and being ready to meet them, to being ready to serve without asking so many questions. When we take the risk of stepping out to serve others, we become a picture for them of the astonishing love of God.

So many times, when I needed it most, it was like having Jesus step into my living room and offer His love and help. Sometimes the biggest answers to prayer come from others who are walking in obedience to Jesus.

And sometimes, I learned, you need to be ready to be the answer to someone's prayer.

24

CECE

And now I must share with you the person who has made the biggest sacrifices for me and my family, and without whom I really don't know how I would have made it through. My sister, Carmen Pitts.

Carmen is my older sister. Though she was older, I spent a lot of my childhood making life a challenge for her. As a kid, I used to pick on her and could sometimes be pretty mean to her. But despite that, she always loved her little brother Jonathan. Thankfully, I finally started to appreciate her. When Wynter and I moved away from New Jersey, she stayed behind. And we didn't often get to spend a lot of time with her, except at family reunions or summer breaks with the larger family. Honestly, I never thought much about it. She was my older sister, whom I dearly loved, but who just wasn't in my life that much anymore.

When the day of the funeral came, all four of my siblings came to be with me. They all made time out of their busy lives to be there and support me. But it was Carmen who pulled me aside to talk privately with me. I didn't really understand at the time how seriously she meant it, but her words were sincere: "Jonathan, I just want you to know that the Lord told me that if you need me, I'll be there. I'll come help you with the girls."

Being the type A achiever that I am, I thought that the offer was kind but unnecessary. We'd be just fine. I simply thanked her and moved on. I didn't want to admit that I needed help at that point. I just figured that if God had prepared me for the task at hand that I would be able to do it…myself.

Two weeks later, the girls and I were in our new home in Franklin, and the girls had settled into their school routines. Anthony Jr. was in town and helping us out by running the girls to school, helping with dinners, and helping us organize our lives. This allowed me to believe everything was under control, but in reality, there was growing chaos just below the surface of our lives.

On the day that Anthony went home, everything changed. I decided to cook a rotisserie chicken and managed to burn it beyond recognition. I'm not a bad cook, but I guess I was just preoccupied and doing my best to hide the pain. The girls thought the burnt chicken was hilarious. I'm sure, though, that in spite of the giggles and smiles, they might have started worrying about the future of our dinners together. I ordered a pizza, and then stumbled upstairs to deal with my humiliation. I stared at the phone for a couple minutes, hesitated, and then dialed Carmen's number. When she answered, I got right to the point.

"Carmen, is that offer still on the table?"

I made that call in the middle of August, about three weeks after Wynter's passing. By Labor Day weekend, Carmen had quit her job, broken her lease, sold her car, and packed up only as many of her belongings as she could fit in two suitcases so that she could fly out to Tennessee and be with us. Carmen had never married and had no children, so it was possible for her to turn her life upside down just like that. When she showed up at the airport, it was almost as if Jesus Himself had come to take care of us. She became the hands and feet of the Lord for the five of us.

Carmen had long prayed for a family, but it hadn't happened for her yet. Now, we would be her family for the time being. She is a person with almost bottomless compassion. She got an advanced degree in counseling and had recently served as a social worker in a residential home for those struggling with mental health issues. I guess all that training came in handy for dealing with us! Another sign of God's sovereign care.

She left her own world and entered into ours, reorganizing our growing chaos without breaking a sweat. She didn't have to work to build trust with the girls since they already knew and loved her. And her contribution to making our home more serene was felt from day one. And at the time, I didn't fully realize yet how the demands of the church, of keeping Wynter's ministry going, and of being a good dad would take so much time.

When she had prayed for a family, I don't think this was what she had in mind, but she stepped in and fully adopted us all into her heart. God certainly knew what we needed, and Carmen fit the bill perfectly.

No more burned chicken. Carmen is a wonderful cook and loves every part of putting a meal together—the planning, the shopping, the prep, and the cooking. Our once scanty refrigerator is filled with great options. And she loves to cook for our visitors as well. As for hospitality, she is second to none.

She quickly picked up the rhythms of our life and adjusted quickly. And then she helped us develop more structure and a higher level of organization. She entered the chaos and turned it into serenity.

She adjusted quickly to the up and down emotions of a grieving family. She was unfailingly patient and compassionate. She knew how to listen and when to stay quiet. She entered into our sorrow and offered the girls total and complete acceptance. On our worst days, she was down with us, but in a healthy way. And on our best days, she rejoiced with us.

In my mind, I can easily picture us all sitting together around the kitchen table. We were a family, and I eventually came to see that she was now part of our immediate family, no longer just a surrogate but a treasured part of us. The girls soon stopped calling her Aunt CeCe, and just started calling her, affectionately, CeCe. She is so much one of us that when we travel without her, or when she takes a vacation on her own, we miss her terribly. Life just isn't the same without her. And when girls need to talk about something sensitive and aren't comfortable sharing it with Dad, they are always comfortable talking openly and honestly with her.

For this part of her life, my sister Carmen has truly become a "helpmate" for me, and I couldn't imagine not having her as part of our close little family.

In the first chapter of Genesis, when God has finished most of His creative work, He looks upon Adam and realizes that something is missing. "The LORD God said, 'It is not good for the man to be alone. I will make a helper suitable for him'" (Genesis 2:18).

I love how God's Word is always breaking down our stereotypes. This word "helpmate" is normally reserved for marriage, and that makes sense. But sometimes God, with His heart for adoption and passion for community, gives it a larger meaning, beyond the boundaries that we can imagine. Of course, there are gaps that Carmen can't fill for me and my girls, but she has plugged more holes than I could ever have imagined. She has been my constant helper.

My life as I know it simply wouldn't be possible without her. Those who don't know the role she plays probably think of me as the grieving dad who likely can't keep up with the demands of housework and all the responsibilities. They probably pity me for the difficulty of such a life. I'd probably deserve all this compassion and pity if it were not for the way that Carmen has seen the needs and stepped in to fill them.

As a pastor and speaker, I have continued to travel and speak, just as I did with Wynter, only now I'm sharing the story of what I have learned through my loss. This wouldn't be possible without Carmen. Because of her, I never have to worry about who is taking care of my beautiful girls. This has allowed me to continue the ministry that Wynter and I once shared with such joy. And Carmen isn't just supporting it; she is part of it.

Sometimes I wonder if Wynter didn't strike a deal with the Lord before she agreed to come home to heaven. I imagine part of the negotiation might have been over granting me a level of support that I could go on without her. If that is true, then Carmen was the answer to those negotiations, and the answer to a prayer I didn't even know I needed to pray.

Carmen remains irreplaceable. Sometimes I ask myself whether, if the shoe was on the other foot, I would be willing to drop everything, turn my life upside down, and serve her in the way she has served me. I hope I would. I want to learn to say yes when God calls on me to meet the needs of someone else.

25

GRIEVING

As a family, our grieving didn't really start until we got settled in Franklin. Following Wynter's death, there didn't seem to be a spare moment for much reflection. There were all the details to attend to, and I just felt shell-shocked. My life seemed to have exploded, and I had taken on all the mental and emotional shrapnel that ripped through what had once been normal. Now nothing in life seemed normal.

One of the things that many people don't realize is that it takes a while for grief to fully manifest itself. At first, you are just dealing with the shock of loss, which leaves you feeling overwhelmed and emotionally numb. Then the grief begins to build in a series of unexpected waves of overpowering emotions.

My grief first presented itself as exhaustion. From the time Wynter passed until we arrived at our new home, I hadn't experienced a complete night of sleep. I awakened early most mornings, my heart aching. Sometimes, in the middle of the night, I startled myself awake and lay there in the dark. I felt so alone, and I worried that Wynter, wherever she was, was experiencing the same feeling of loneliness.

I was sometimes wracked by irrational guilt. I worried that I had failed her. Wherever she was, I could no longer be there for her. And I wondered if I might somehow be at fault. I wrestled with these feelings.

Could I have done more? Why wasn't I more sensitive to the excessive tired-
ness she had been feeling? Why didn't I see the signs? Should I have slowed
down the moving process? Had I somehow, unintentionally, created a level
of stress that her heart simply couldn't cope with? I had gone to see a counselor in Dallas just a few days after her death, and he helped me see
that it was irrational to blame myself. Even as grief washed over me, I
knew that these thoughts were not rational, but it still didn't keep me
from wrestling with them.

What we say to ourselves in the process of grieving is of critical
importance in our recovery. I'd learned long ago not to let myself
dwell on irrational thoughts, and now that knowledge was extremely
helpful as I struggled with my thoughts and feelings. I'd memorized
2 Corinthians 10:5 (NASB), which says "We are destroying speculations
and every lofty thing raised up against the knowledge of God, and we
are taking every thought captive to the obedience of Christ."

Paul was suggesting a strategy of taking every thought captive and not
letting idle speculations take control. He knew from experience that one
of the greatest weapons the enemy has to use against us is our negative
self-talk. When you begin to believe the lies and allow yourself to focus
on thoughts that aren't from God, you will soon find yourself overcome
by them. Instead, Paul encouraged his readers in the church at Corinth
to replace those lies with the truth about God and about themselves as it
is revealed in the Scriptures. We tend to live in accordance with how we
are thinking about ourselves. If we can't control our thought life, we open
ourselves up for trouble. Instead, we need to fill our mind with truth.

So, when a question arose in my mind, such as *Could I have done*
more? I would simply call to mind a truth that I knew from the Bible
and hold on to that. Instead of climbing aboard a carousel of self-
incrimination, I would remind myself of how Jesus thought about me:

"Indeed, the very hairs of your head are all numbered. Don't be
afraid; you are worth more than many sparrows" (Luke 12:7).

Or,

"Jesus said to her, 'I am the resurrection and the life. The one who
believes in me will live, even though they die; and whoever lives by
believing in me will never die'" (John 11:25-26).

Or,

"The righteous perish, and no one takes it to heart; the devout are taken away, and no one understands that the righteous are taken away to be spared from evil. Those who walk uprightly enter into peace; they find rest as they lie in death" (Isaiah 57:1-2).

These and many other scriptures, some of which I had learned as a child, reminded me of the truth even as the enemy whispered lies into my ears. If there was anything that helped me to think in healthy ways during my time of grieving, it was the Word of God, which kept me steadied every time it felt like my world was shaking and unstable. His Word was my stability. Embracing these truths kept me in a place of trust and belief and helped me put aside all the feelings of guilt and shame.

One of the best strategies for me was singing the words of truth. I love singing. I sing in the shower. I sing when I am working with my hands. I sing, sometimes at the top of my voice, when I am driving. When I married Wynter, I sang to her at the wedding ceremony, and I sang to her as she was passing away. And, snuggling down near Wynter's tummy, I had sung to each of my daughters while they were still in the womb. When I had to tell them of their mother's death, I sang to them again.

I believe in the power of song, especially songs which rise to God in gratitude and praise. I'm committed to consistently, audibly, and loudly lifting my voice, even when I don't feel it. A song can be a powerful declaration of faith.

In my midtwenties, I had even taken the concept of taking every thought captive and made it into a song. Throughout the years, I have sung it to myself whenever I needed a reminder not to listen to the enemy's lies. God once again demonstrated His sovereign grace in that I rediscovered the lyrics to this song I had written while in the process of moving. And once again, they brought comfort and confirmation. I even got up the courage to post myself singing this little song on Instagram in the hope that it could help others. Looking at that video today, I can see the hurt and pain in my eyes, but I can also see the settled trust in God:

God, you've been so faithful,
Lord, you've been so good,
When everything was going wrong,
    your faithfulness showed through.
Lord, your faithfulness, your faithfulness,
    your faithfulness showed through.
Lord, your faithfulness, your faithfulness,
    your faithfulness showed through.
God, you've been so faithful,
Lord, you've been so good,
When everything was going right,
    your faithfulness shined through.

Not long ago, I framed these words and hung them on my bedroom wall, just as surely as I have framed them in my heart and mind. They serve as a constant reminder that God is faithful and good at all times—when things are going well, and when they are a struggle. No matter how unsteady I might feel, God is always steady and faithful. He is always there.

———

Early on, I thought I was doing better in the grieving process than most people usually do. But soon I discovered that I was just like everyone else. Despite all my natural optimism, I learned that I was not immune from experiencing many of the same things that are common among those who are grieving. Here are a few of the unexpected losses that occurred for me.

One of the things that happened is that I lost my appetite. It didn't matter what you put down in front of me, including favorites like a Philly Cheese Steak sandwich or a box of Hot Tamales, both of which I had often craved. During my season of grief, neither of these tasted good. Nor did anything else. I just lost interest in eating, which is a common experience for those who are grieving. Consequently, in a month or so of Wynter's passing, I lost about 20 pounds. I was already pretty lean, so this was a loss not only of some fat, but also of some muscle mass.

Another thing I lost was muscle tone. My desire to work out and keep fit seemed to disappear. Once I had averaged three to four workouts per week and loved running, lifting weights, and doing exercises. Suddenly, I was down to maybe three times a month. Working out seemed pointless and futile, and I lost interest in doing it. The only thing that got me to make an occasional visit to the gym was the prodding of my oldest daughter.

I also lost interest in some of the things I enjoyed most. For me, that was watching sports on television. It was a rare weekend when I wasn't tuned in to a game. I'll never forget that earlier in the year of Wynter's death, I watched my home team, the Philadelphia Eagles, win the Super Bowl with my family in Baltimore. Honestly, it was the last game I wholeheartedly enjoyed. While my father and I were glued to the game in the basement, Wynter had crept upstairs and overheard my three youngest daughters talking about the Super Bowl.

While the game could be heard in the background, Kaitlyn asked, with a bit of a superior tone, "What's the point of the Super Bowl?"

Camryn was quick with a response: "Somebody wins."

Kaitlyn asked a follow-up: "Wins what?"

Then Camryn's twin sister, Olivia, shot out with one word: "Money."

Kaitlyn, still unimpressed, rolled her eyes. "But why do we care? We're not getting the money!"

They all started to giggle, and Olivia shrugged and said, "People just like to watch it."

Indeed, people do. And that day, we did. It seemed as though the fate of the world, or at least our happiness, rested on whether the Eagles would prevail. For the moment, it was everything to us. The Eagles were on the cusp of victory, and we were hooked.

But now football games just couldn't keep my attention. After all I had been through, losing the love of my life, the game I had once loved so passionately just seemed kind of pointless.

I think that Solomon was saying about the same thing as my girls were saying when he evaluated the values of all our entertainments: "It is better to go to a house of mourning than to go to a house of feasting, for death is the destiny of everyone; the living should take this to heart"

(Ecclesiastes 7:2). In other words, though there is a lot of stuff we like to do in life, we must keep it all in perspective. When we are partying and feasting, it is easy to place too much importance on these things. But death changes our perception of what really matters most in life.

I never lost interest in being a good father for my girls. They remained the most important things in my life. I never lost interest in friendship and family. All my relationships had grown stronger in the face of my loss. I never lost interest in the things of God. In fact, I started to see that all these things were even more of a priority than I had valued them before.

I'm not saying football is bad or a waste of time. Neither is going shopping for clothes. Or whatever your favorite pastime might be. But you begin to realize where they actually stand on the list of most important things when you go through the refining process of grieving. Your values change or at least are confirmed. In the process of grieving, God has a way of getting your attention.

26

EMOTIONS

I've always loved something I once heard Tony Evans say: "Emotions do not have intellect. Emotions don't think." This concept was so helpful to me as I went through the ups and downs of how I was feeling during my deepest period of grief. I thank God that during this period I was able to see a really good counselor, who helped me find words for the things I was feeling and helped me think through my emotional turmoil. If I had just relied on my emotional state, I would really have struggled.

Note to anyone who is facing a similar crisis in their life: Don't be afraid to get some help. Don't be too proud to find someone who can help you keep your perspective during a dark time in your life.

We have to be careful about our emotions. They can be helpful when they work like a thermometer to give us a read on how we are doing. They can let us know when we are "overheated" and need to cool down. But they can become a problem when they operate like a thermostat, where they dictate, drive, and control us.

As Dr. Evans always said, faith should operate *in spite of* our feelings. Our faith should be the thermostat and keep our emotions from raging out of control. It all comes down to what we believe and who we trust. "Faith," says Dr. Evans, "is simply acting like God is telling the truth." That is, in my opinion, the best definition of faith I have ever heard.

So, when it comes to grieving, I refused to believe the lie that I'd never be happy again.

I refused to believe the lie that somehow Wynter's premature death was my fault.

I refused to believe the lie that God didn't love us enough to allow Wynter and me to have many more years together.

I refused to believe the lie that everything that happened was just the result of blind chance.

Instead, I choose to believe that the God who loves me and has everything in control still is in charge. His timing is perfect. His love is forever. And He still has a plan for my life.

Even when my emotions tell a different story, by faith I can believe the story that God has written for me.

I'm a planner. I focus on the positive and keep moving forward. That's my natural tendency. I like to dwell on the positive and see the silver lining in every cloud. In many ways, this has helped me walk through my grief in a good way.

But...

One of the things I had to learn is not to rush it. Not to move beyond my grief too quickly. But to stop and listen and let it teach me what I needed to know. Not to skip over the steps of deep and honest grieving that are a part of healing the pain.

I wanted to run toward the future, assuming that God had already worked everything out. But honestly, I discovered that the last thing I should do is get there before Him! Sometimes the path of healing requires some baby steps, and if we get in a rush, it just isn't a good thing. And grief isn't a path we were meant to walk alone.

Along the path of grief, my counselor helped me understand some things about myself that I'm not certain I would have really discovered without her help.

I learned that I am a perfectionist. That my mind is quick to judge and criticize every move I make, but that my heart is where my hope lives. That sometimes when the two are in tension, I need to trust my gut, slow down, and take my time.

Another person who counseled me, someone on staff at the new church, helped me understand that when I was in a state of grief, everything was a little bit exaggerated inside me. I was like an old wagon train in the wild, wild West, and my temperament and my zeal were more like a racehorse, ready to plunge ahead. Racehorses, he reminded me, are not good for pulling wagons. My daughters were the four wheels of that wagon, wobbling as I tried to race ahead.

The path out of grief was meant to be a slow and steady journey in a fragile wagon, not a race to the destination of being okay. My counselor helped me realize that the faster I tried to pull ahead, the more unsteady the wagon would be. And since my daughters were part of that wagon, I was putting them at risk when I tried to get better too quickly. If I didn't slow down, they might just come loose themselves. My steadfastness would be their steadfastness. Or my speed might jolt them loose. That illustration single-handedly forced me to reevaluate some of the ways I had been thinking and acting.

He continued to explain to me that depression comes when we dwell too much on the past, and anxiety comes when we press too quickly toward the future. The middle way was a slow and steady journey. He encouraged me to see that God doesn't exist in the past or the future, but is here with me in the present, ready to meet me and walk alongside me in the here and now…moment by moment.

I had to think differently.

I'll always have my memories with Wynter. I treasure them beyond words. But I can't allow myself to live in the memories. I can visit them, but I need to bring the joy from them into the now, or they might just drag me down. Neither can I just move on as quickly as possible.

I need to "be still." In this moment and every moment, walking in trust as He guides me toward healing from the loss.

27

GRATITUDE

Part of being still meant learning to rest. And by God's grace and the church's gift, I did just that. I took six weeks of sabbatical, which was honestly the first sabbatical I had ever taken. I learned so much during those six weeks.

I learned how to rest, which is something I have never really been very good at. But in those somber six weeks, I put everything stressful aside and pursued some quiet. I slept late and took several naps every day. Other times, when I needed to calm myself, I would just go sit quietly for 10 or 15 minutes, doing nothing but listening in silence.

Silence, I found, was the first step for getting rid of anxious thoughts, fears, and irrational responses. Sometimes, during one of these times of silence, I would drift off to sleep, which was okay because I needed it. Sometimes, I would pray the simplest kinds of prayers. Prayers of child-like honesty and trust. And sometimes, I meditated on scriptures that I knew, letting God teach me from the words I had memorized long ago.

More than anything else, it was in the silence that I discovered how grateful I was for my life. For Wynter and the years we were blessed to have together. She was like a gift that was unwrapped over time, and the more years we had together, the more grateful I was for how God had shown His love for me through her.

One day I came across a letter that she had written to me during a marriage retreat we had attended called *A Weekend to Remember*. Honestly, that had been a tough weekend. We weren't in the best spot at that point. Some tensions had bubbled up in our marriage, and now we were being asked to address them with honesty. One of the exercises of the weekend was to write a letter to our spouse.

I plopped down on the bed to read what she had written. I couldn't help but weep as I reread her honest words. Tears of sadness mixed with the deepest kind of gratitude that I'd been privileged to have her in my life—this wonderful, complicated, but amazing woman.

As I sat there, there was a stillness that came over me, and I felt enveloped in a warm silence, the presence of God so very real in that moment.

I began to think about all I had to be grateful for, even now in the midst of my pain. Of course, my deepest gratitude was just that I had been able to have the years I did with Wynter. But there was more to be thankful for.

I was grateful for my daughters. Each of them a spitting image of their mother, but each so unique in their personalities and gifts. I could see so many of her qualities spread among my girls. Thankfully, her heart, which could have given way at any point, had not failed before she had a chance to see them growing up into beautiful young women. She'd experienced their fourteenth, twelfth, and ninth birthdays. She had seen each of them baptized into faith. And the books she had written were written with them in mind. They were her first and most important audience. She had the chance to see them get excited about her growing ministry, and she had made an incalculable impact on each of their lives. Her legacy has made them who they are today, and I couldn't be prouder of them.

I was grateful for the ministry we had developed together. It was her baby, but I threw myself into it with full confidence in the way that God was using her, but also using us. We wrote a parenting book together, which was easy and fun, and a marriage book together, which was hard and caused us both to grow in unexpected ways. Ultimately, our life together was our ministry. Everything we learned in our own marriage and parenting we had the opportunity and blessing to share with others.

And I was grateful to God. Even though I wouldn't have chosen this path, it is one that I don't have to walk alone. He gave me strength and courage, and He picked me up each time I fell or failed.

So, during this season of sorrow, it was just as much a season of worship. Nothing I could do would bring my best friend back. Nothing I could say would explain everything to my girls or fully assure them that everything would be okay. This was a time of trust and a time to worship God in the middle of what I was going through. My life was, and still is, a life of complete reliance on the Lord.

As I lifted my voice in worship, I was thankful for what we'd had, and I was ready for what lay in store in the future. I can't tell you how many times I listened to the song "Do It Again"—a song that spoke of being in desperate places and remembering that God would never fail us. It's a song that we'd often sing along to as a family when we took a drive, sat at the dinner table, or joined the congregation during a worship service. But now it took on a special relevance and a deeper meaning for me. It was the anthem of our hearts as we laid Wynter to rest and as we walked together into an unknown future. As the song says, "I'm still in Your hands."

We don't have to be in control of everything. We can leave everything in His hands. We can rest in His presence and His promises. We can cling to Him as He does for us what we cannot do for ourselves.

Gratitude has a powerful way of bringing healing to your soul. I could have sulked over what I had lost, but being thankful gave me the peace I needed and the reasons to keep on the path of faith and faithfulness.

28

UNCLE INSANITY

Our first Thanksgiving after Wynter's passing was one I'll never forget. Most of my family and a lot of my friends descended upon our home to share the holiday with us. It was weird and a bit sad to be celebrating without having Wynter present, but mostly I was overcome by the love and support that each of the people who came offered me and my girls. Everyone sacrificed their time and money to be present, as some had to travel quite a distance to be there.

Being my normal type A self, though, I was worried about all the details. For most of them, this would be the very first time they would see our new home. Honestly, I imagined some of them didn't expect much, knowing all that we had walked through. I wanted to prove them wrong. I also wanted to project an attitude of strength. I was convinced that I wouldn't need as much time to grieve as most people did, and I was certainly not going to bother them with how I was feeling if I started to feel sad.

As people began to arrive, I began to get stressed. Many of them would be staying here for five days, and I didn't want my nine young nieces and nephews to touch my newly painted white walls. Instead of just accepting the reality that kids having fun means a few smears and stains, and that I could always touch things up afterwards, I slipped into control freak mode, hovering over them like Uncle Insanity. My life had been so out of control for several months that I wanted this week to be calm and controlled. When I wasn't policing for fingerprints and moving breakable objects out of reach, I was straightening up behind everyone—adults as well as the kids. I slaved to keep every room tidy and every dish washed.

When I wasn't stressing everyone else out with my obsessiveness, I retreated to the bedroom to find some peace and quiet from all the noise and chaos that ruled the house that week. I don't think I was much fun to be around, but thankfully, they are a very forgiving bunch.

When it was all over, I breathed a sigh of relief and imagined that everyone had a good time. But then I got a call from my twin brother who was a bit offended by my unwillingness to just relax and enjoy the opportunity to be with his kids. Ben even shared that his kids thought I was mean to them. I was shocked and offended, using my own pain as my excuse for my behavior.

A similar experience followed at Easter, and I'm kind of surprised they even wanted to celebrate with me. This was followed by a similar conversation, similar excuses, and a similar sense of righteous offense on my part. But deep inside, I knew that it was wrong for me to use my grief as an excuse for what was just plain obsessiveness and unkindness on my part. I must add that I'm still trying to recover my reputation with a few of my nieces. They recently called me the "grumpy uncle." But I will win them back!

I would come to realize that what was important wasn't the house, or my immediate mood, but the need to be present with the people I loved. I didn't want to push them away or treat them as a nuisance. I knew I needed to show up for them no matter how I might be feeling. I started to grieve over what I was becoming in the process of grieving, and I determined to change that.

I've continued to grow in this area. It is always easier for me to try to control people and situations than just to be fully present with them. In this case, I needed to understand that they were grieving as well, and they needed me as much as I needed them.

My greatest teacher for learning how to deal with this was my coworker and free counselor, Jack. He kept emphasizing that I need to focus on the present and upon being present with others. When God wanted to reveal Himself to us, Jack reminded me, He didn't send a telegram or make a phone call or require us to search Him out, He came to us in the person of Jesus. God was present to us in Jesus, and that was the example I needed to follow.

The truth I learned about myself that Thanksgiving week is that I was scared. Without Wynter, I didn't really know who I was anymore. This was something that would take time and trust to figure out, and a lot of listening to God, but I knew I didn't want to be the unfriendly Mr. Clean that I'd been that week. Thankfully, I had a very supportive and forgiving family who were willing to be patient with me while I learned these lessons. And I had a God who understood me and was willing to work with me just exactly as I was, moving closer to becoming what He desired me to be.

⟶•⟵

Grief takes so much out of a person. The problem is that it also can take a lot out of the people you love. The process has been tough not only on me, but also on my girls. There's a lesson here: Everyone needs to have some patience and some forbearance with those who are suffering alongside you. And you need to keep aware of the impact of your emotional ups and downs, especially upon the younger children in your life.

As I have walked through all the stages of this journey, my girls have seen the worst in me. They've watched my occasional inability to cope manifest itself through being frustrated and short-tempered about the smallest things. A light thoughtlessly left on, or a typical argument between two siblings could sometimes set off a response all out of proportion to the crime. Sometimes I wanted to escape and be alone at just the time when one of them really needed to talk with me. Other times I rushed them over a meal or a shopping trip because I hit some sort of emotional wall and couldn't handle things very well. And my innate self-centeredness raised its ugly head when I didn't really give enough thought to how they were feeling.

Maybe I'm being too hard on myself, but I think that a good dad needs to keep the needs of his children in mind, not just his own needs. And that is especially true during a time like this. Of course, they've been devastated by it, but I was amazed at their strength.

God has been gracious to me, and so have my girls. Overall, I am amazed at how well they have handled this painful disruption to their lives. What I learned from them during this time is that we all have to be there for each other.

29

SISSY

One of the greatest gifts I received during this time in my life was the willingness of a counselor to help my children walk through their grief in a way I never could have provided. Wynter had gotten to know Sissy Goff on a speaking circuit they both traveled and when she was interviewed by Wynter for her podcast. Wynter was immediately drawn to Sissy's wisdom, her heart, and her caring way with words. One of the great things about moving to the Nashville area was that Sissy was part of a counseling practice nearby. When she heard what had happened, Sissy was quick to offer her help for the girls.

When we first entered the doors of Daystar Counseling, we knew we were in a special place. Everything about it was calming and reassuring. The smell of popcorn and cider wafted down the halls, and there were cozy rocking chairs waiting on the front porch. Plus, there were puppies, whose enthusiastic welcome made everybody know this was a loving and accepting place.

Over the weeks and months, Sissy helped them work through their feelings, never rushing them and always treating them with understanding and respect. They could open up to her in a way that they really couldn't with their dad. She felt like family. In fact, we've featured her in *For Girls Like You* magazine and shared other ministry opportunities over the years. There aren't words enough to describe how much she has helped our family and how much her peaceful presence has brought peace to us.

—◈—

In the early days of Wynter's passing, I thought that grief was something that I had to get through and that accomplishment would be measured by how quickly I found myself on the other side of it. I thought of it as a battle that I needed to win. I didn't want to be defeated by it. I was going to, if necessary, beat grief into submission.

That was just a mixture of pride and pragmatism. I thought I was strong, and I wanted to get past all the pain as soon as I could. I trusted in my logical way of thinking about things, figured I would allow myself a sufficient amount of time to grieve, and then I would be better. But grief doesn't work that way.

I remember the shock I felt when I was talking to another pastor and telling him about my plans to keep Wynter's ministry alive. I had it all mapped out in my head. Then suddenly, in the middle of explaining, I started to weep. "I don't want to fail my wife," I said through the tears.

I had placed two huge burdens on myself. First, that I would get through the grief process as rapidly as I could. And second, that I would keep Wynter's ministry going without a hitch. I suddenly realized that I just couldn't do either alone. I needed to be weak enough to ask for God's strength.

Now I understand that grief is a long and winding journey that won't end until the day I am perfected in the presence of Jesus.

30

SHE IS YOURS

I now know that I'll be continually going back to God in weakness, day after day. One evening in late March, eight months after Wynter graduated to heaven, I was walking by the bedroom of one of my daughters. I could hear her softly crying. I gently pushed the door open and went inside, where I knelt next to the bed. "What's wrong, sweetie?" I asked.

As though I didn't know.

Her response was simple, and totally from her heart: "I miss Mommy."

"Me too, honey." I wanted her to be assured that I knew what she was feeling. And, for once, I was smart enough not to say anything else, but just to sit with her in silence. Just to be there with her.

Then came words that I wasn't prepared for. She gently whispered, "I'm having a hard time believing that God is real." My stomach dropped. I wasn't prepared for this. "And if He is real," she continued, "I'm having a hard time believing that He is good."

I honestly didn't know exactly how to respond. I knew this wasn't a good time for an apologetics lecture on the evidence for God's reality. But somehow, I couldn't help myself, and I started giving her answers and assurances that didn't have a gentle tone. I realized that I was actually kind of angry at her for her doubts and afraid that she was losing her faith.

When I left her room, I was still shaken. Was it perhaps that I wasn't

willing to be honest with myself about my own questions and struggles? Afraid that if I admitted to the slightest doubt that all the confidence in God that I was leaning on would come tumbling down? How
could our family hold together if some of us couldn't trust and believe?

———

Then I remembered what I had been learning about codependence,
about letting someone else's emotional struggles affect your own emotional well-being. And it hit me. I had a codependent relationship with
my daughters. I expected them to grieve like I grieved, and think like I
thought, and relate to God in the same way that I did. I was so focused
on making sure they felt happy and secure and didn't experience too
much pain that I wasn't letting them find their own path through. I
wasn't comfortable with letting them struggle with God as they might
need to. Bottom line is that I wasn't releasing them to God's care.

I thought about the prayer which was in the book Wynter and I had
written about parenting called *She Is Yours: Trusting God as You Raise
the Girl He Gave You.* Now my own words and the prayer that Wynter and I had co-labored to create came back to minister to my heart:

> Dear God,
> I release my daughter in Your care.
> I surrender my desire to control her.
> I surrender my desire to manipulate her future.
> I surrender my tendency to overprotect,
>   shelter, and suffocate her.
> I surrender my desire to be her best friend, first.
> I surrender my own dreams for her.
> I surrender my need to be her source.
> She is Yours.
> I'm totally open to You, dependent upon You,
>   and desperate for You to be in control as I let go.
> I'm relying on the fact that You are God and that You
>   have created my daughter for Your purpose and
>   for this time.

I pray that You will draw her to Yourself.
I pray that she will delight in You.
I pray that You will be patient with her.
I pray that You will provide for her.
I pray that You will bless her.
I pray that You will use her to be a blessing to others.
I pray that You will mature her.
And ultimately, I pray that she will show Jesus
 in her very being.
I trust in Your sovereignty; I wait in expectation
 for Your providence.
Lord, she is Yours, and I trust You with her. Amen.

————

Wynter and I had framed this prayer and hung it on the wall to be a reminder to us of God's faithful love for our girls. That He loved them even more than we did. And it was the reminder this codependent dad needed just now. I lifted it off the wall, wrote my daughter's name on the back of the canvas, dated it, and hung it back in its place.

I left my codependence on the inside of that canvas and submitted it to the Lord. I once again gave all my daughters back to the Lord and trusted Him to show Himself to them and walk with them through their grief. I trusted Him to know how to deal with their doubts and questions. And I continue to pull down that canvas and sign and date it whenever I'm tempted to take back control from God.

By God's grace, my daughter wasn't scarred by these moments. I actually apologized to her the next day. She forgave me, and I began the process of letting her go from my iron grip. I've watched all of them struggle and recover, only to see them struggle and recover again. In the end, I've seen the Holy Spirit's work in each of their lives, and I'm confident that they will overcome despite the continuing battle they'll likely face until they are in the perfect presence of God, just like their mom.

31

LEARNING TO LEAN

My twin brother and I sang in a gospel quartet during our college years. We learned many of the great Negro spirituals and other hymns that have carried the message that has stuck with me ever since. One that has moved me the most is "Learning to Lean," a song that talks about the need to lean on Jesus to get us through all we face in our lives. Learning to lean on Him hasn't always been easy, especially in my days of grieving, but I've realized it is the only posture I can afford to have if I want to find peace, and it's the only one that will allow me to walk through this life with God's grace. As Proverbs 3:5-6 recommends, "Trust in the Lord with all your heart and lean not on your own understanding; in all your ways submit to him, and he will make your paths straight."

In whatever you might be going through, my friend, remember that you don't have to go through it alone. Jesus is just waiting for you to lean into His love so He can be the strength that will get you through. I can assure you this is true, because this is what I have learned during my own journey through grief.

32

HOME IS WHERE GOD IS

When Wynter died, I knew two things instinctively:
First, that she was home. I knew that she had crossed the threshold as a traveler from this world to the next. She was with Jesus, and heaven was her place of residence. She didn't pass into nothingness but opened the door to eternity. She didn't belong to me. She belonged to the Lord, and now He had come to take her home. It was only the realization of this truth that gave me the strength to let go. I hated having to go on without her, and her absence brings a deep loneliness and sadness to me. Sometimes this absence still catches me unaware with its emotional upheaval. But I know that isn't the end of our story.

Second, I knew that even without her, I too was home. As the psalmist reminds us, "Lord, through all the generations you have been our home!" (Psalm 90:1 NLT) The pages of the Bible are filled with reminders of such a hope. God is our dwelling place, our home. And, we are, as Paul reminds us, a home for God: "Do you not know that you are a temple of God and that the Spirit of God dwells in you?" (1 Corinthians 3:16 NASB). He lives inside us. Through His Spirit, He makes His home with us.

Even when Wynter's absence is most real to me, I am reminded that she is with God, and that God is with me. She is in perfect peace in His presence, and I am still on that journey to the place where we will see each other again.

This is the peace that gets me through even the darkest of days.

———

If you were to ask me the basis of my faith, and how I can trust in God even when the unexpected happens, I would be able to boil it all down to a simple statement: "I've tasted and seen that God is good." This is my paraphrase of one of my favorite Bible verses: "Taste and see that the LORD is good; blessed is the one who takes refuge in him" (Psalm 34:8). I have experienced the blessing that comes when God is my safe place during the storms of life.

He is good in the good times.

But He is also good in the bad times.

When my world came crashing down around me, some people wondered how a good God could take away a beloved spouse with no warning, or how a good God could decide to separate four little girls from their mother.

With confidence and compassion, I can say to them, and to myself, and to you, my reader: Yes, He is good.

That is the message that rings through every page of this book. Even when we don't understand it, He is working for our good. "All things work together for good to those who love God, to those who are the called according to His purpose" (Romans 8:28 NKJV). All things. God doesn't occasionally make a mistake and let tragedy slip through. No, He is weaving everything that happens to us into a tapestry that ultimately shines forth His goodness and care.

His goodness comes in surprising moments of grace, in the tenderness of friends, and in the unaccountable peace I often find in the stillness and silence. He has not forsaken me or forgotten me. He has been there to lead and guide as well as comfort and console me.

He is THAT good.

33

SAYING YES

I used to think that living a life of purpose for God involved a lot of things I needed to do: be obedient, plan and strategize wisely, memorize His Word, find courage to follow Him, speak to others about Him, understand His plan, listen to His call. On and on the list could go. And these are all good things. But they aren't the main thing. If you really want to be used by God, there is one primary thing you need to do: Say yes.

All God really needs from you is your willingness. He doesn't need your talents or your energy level or your positive outlook. He just needs you to be available.

In my 15 years of being married to Wynter, we learned this lesson again and again. I had a front-row seat for seeing what God could do when a person was willing to say yes.

When you are willing to say yes, you can put aside all the striving and second-guessing, and all the worrying about whether you are pleasing God or finding His purpose.

Our place and our purpose are found in that little three-letter word.

And during the days of grief, I learned again and again that the path to healing and wellness came from my willingness to follow. To say yes.

34

TENTS

We are all on a journey. Each of us is traveling through life, and every one of us has a special and unique purpose that God has entrusted to us. How well we navigate that journey depends on recognizing that it *is* a journey, that the frustrations and challenges and disappointments of today, whatever they may be, are not the final story. God loves to redeem stories, even those that might feel hopeless at any particular moment along the way. He is the greatest Author, and He isn't done writing your story or mine. So, as we keep moving forward with Him, we need to remember that the final destination for those who place their hope in Christ is not the grave, that God has a life for us beyond this one.

Sometimes, especially when we are young, it's easy to forget that we are mortal and that each of our lives will eventually end. We tend to focus on today and try not to think too much about the fact that someday we will die—every single one of us. Through losing Wynter, death became much more of a reality to me. It was no longer an abstract idea. It was real—a reminder that someday my own life on this earth will come to an end, and that when that time comes, God has a place prepared especially for me. As Paul writes, "For we know that if the earthly tent we live in is destroyed, we have a building from God, an eternal house in heaven, not built by human hands" (2 Corinthians 5:1).

These words from the Bible line up with the reality of life as I have experienced it. The body we live in is like a tent—not a permanent dwelling, but a temporary shelter. Even if your own "tent" is in pretty good shape, it is only a place to dwell on this particular part of your journey. It isn't your final destination. There is a better home awaiting.

Growing up, I was an Eagle Scout, and my favorite part of being a scout was to go camping and to pitch my tent in all kinds of places. I enjoyed the sights and smells of the great outdoors and found peace and joy in nature. Whether it was the finger lakes of New York, the mountains of New Mexico, or the beautiful Appalachian Trail, I loved it all. I learned how to put up a tent quickly and efficiently, and then how to take it down. The tents my scout troop used were a bright red in color and barnlike in shape. You could fit two full-sized cots inside, and you could stand up straight inside of their large metal frame scaffolding. Our tents were more eye-catching than those of a lot of other scouts—not the typical boring pup tent. They were roomy and comfortable, and they did a good job of protecting us from the elements. And they looked cool—at least as cool as a tent can look! At times we weathered some pretty severe storms in our tents—storms that would tend to make a normal pup tent collapse in a heap.

When I was 13 years old, my troop attended the National Boy Scout Jamboree. Scouts from all over the country came to Fort A.P. Hill in Virginia and set up their tents, which seemed to stretch as far as the eye could see. There were few buildings in sight on the giant field where we pitched camp. This event was the "Super Bowl" of scouting—a week-long opportunity to hone our skills and meet scouts from various parts of the United States.

One evening, as we relaxed around our tents, a sudden summer storm blew through with such intensity that it whipped up a sort of whirlwind, which tore through the camp, pelting us with severe wind, heavy rain, and thundering clouds. By morning, the sturdy red tents of my troop were just about the only ones left standing!

But even our tents, built to withstand the punishments of weather and the decaying effect of time, eventually became less dependable. I doubt that any of those incredibly durable barn tents are still in commission today. These tents are like our bodies. Mine outlasted Wynter's, and yours may outlast mine, but none of our bodies are going to last forever. Eventually, the storm of death is going to make them only a memory.

The good news is that you are not just your body. Your soul resides in the tent of your body, and that soul is meant to last forever. Your soul is traveling through time, and it just happens to be housed in your body for now. The apostle Paul, himself a tentmaker by occupation, knew something about where the real you and the real me resides, and the future that lies before us when we finally shed our own "tents": "We are confident, I say, and would prefer to be away from the body and at home with the Lord" (2 Corinthians 5:8).

No matter how much I loved spending time in a tent as a scout, when the trip was over, I was ready to come home and sleep in the comfort of my bed at home. You and I are not meant to live in these "tents" forever; we look forward to our home in heaven—a place where we will be with the Lord forever.

I know Wynter is home now. The moment she left this earth, Wynter went to be with Jesus. She was relocated to the very presence of God. I miss her terribly, and I think of her every day, but I know she is well, and she is with Him. One day, I will join her there.

You might be tempted to think that none of this is really relevant to you right now, and you might put off thinking about your eternal home until you are older and closer to your own day of reckoning. Wynter and I never imagined that the storm of death would blow through our lives and take her at such an early age. There are no guarantees in this life. I've learned that keeping the possibility of death in front of you is a good way to keep yourself focused on the things beyond this life.

You and I are both traveling from our temporary home to a final destination, and God wants to be your companion on that journey. And if He is your companion, it means that you can be at home, right now, wherever you are. Whatever storms blow through your life, you can be assured that He is there with you. You've probably heard the saying, "The journey is the destination." When you are walking with God, you can find peace and comfort and purpose *right now*. In 2 Corinthians 5:9, Paul continues: "So we make it our goal to please him, whether we are at home in the body or away from it." As my good friend Rebekah Lyons wrote in her book *You Are Free*, "Home is wherever God is and God is ever with me."[6] That is a comforting thought as we journey through life. Even if our temporary tent gets the worst of it through the blustering tempests, we are at home with Him, even now.

God is in heaven, yes. Therefore, heaven is home. But God can be with you and me right *now*.

Moses, certainly a man who knew what it meant to travel, one who lived in tents and was well acquainted with the trials of a long and arduous journey, wrote these words in a psalm which most scholars believe came from his hand: "He who dwells in the shelter of the Most High will abide in the shadow of the Almighty. I will say to the Lord, 'My refuge and my fortress, my God in whom I trust'" (Psalm 91:1-2 ESV). And, as the apostle Paul reminds us, God doesn't just dwell *with* us; He dwells *in* us. He prays, "That He would grant you, according to the riches of His glory, to be strengthened with might through His Spirit in the inner man, that *Christ may dwell in your hearts* through faith" (Ephesians 3:16-17 NKJV, italics added).

This is one of most important things that has been confirmed in my heart through the whole experience of losing Wynter. I hope, through my stories, to share the comfort and peace I have found in the midst of grieving. I'm confident that you'll be reminded that God is our true home. He has the power to help you through any hardship, loss, pain, or difficulty, just as He has done for me. He will be your shelter—your home—through every step of the way.

> God is our refuge and strength, an ever-present help in trouble. Therefore, we will not fear, though the earth give way and the mountains fall into the heart of the sea, though its waters roar and foam and the mountains quake with their surging (Psalm 46:1-3).

35

WYNTER'S PROMISE

Throughout my life with Wynter, the one thing she struggled with from time to time was a question she could never really put into words, but which was essentially, Does my life matter? Or, its related question: Does what I do matter?

Even as her ministry grew, Wynter still struggled with these feelings. Her response was to memorize a lot of Scripture so that she could bring it to mind whenever this self-doubt arose. Honestly, I think this is a battle almost every one of us faces from time to time—the nagging question of whether we are making a difference in our life.

Wynter's solution was a good one. She wrote down scriptures on 3 x 5 cards and used a sticky note to place them all over the house. She had some on her mirrors, some in her closet, some in her purse, and some in her minivan. I'd come across them constantly, and I was always proud of her for filling her mind with God's words to combat the lies that she might otherwise be believing about herself.

⸺⸺

About 14 months after her death, I was sitting at my desk in my home office in Tennessee, and Wynter was very much on my mind. A heaviness swept over me, as I was missing her something fierce. So, I

177

was letting my mind travel back over some of the great memories we had made together, which was always a good way to replace some of the sadness with gratitude.

It was then that I noticed a bright pink 3 x 5 card attached to the side of the small wooden bookshelf in the office. Somehow, I had never noticed it before. It was a decorative bookshelf that seemed kind of out of place here, but I'd never found another place for it. And I didn't have the heart to toss it since it was a shelf for the books she used in her ministry work.

I leaned backward at kind of an odd angle to read what was written there in Wynter's bold and slightly messy handwriting: "You did not choose me, but I chose you and appointed you that you should go and bear fruit and that your fruit should abide, so that whatever you ask the Father in my name, he may give to you" (John 15:16).

I couldn't help myself. I just started to cry. I knew how much this verse had meant to Wynter, and somehow it had survived our move, just waiting for me to discover it. This was the verse that, more than any other, Wynter held onto when she began to have questions about whether what she was doing really mattered. It reminded her that God had custom built and designed the work she was doing for young girls, *especially for her and her daughters*. That God was using her to bear fruit, even in those times when she couldn't really see it.

This verse comes from John 15, where Jesus uses the illustration of a vineyard to teach His disciples about how God works to prune and perfect us for the good of His Kingdom. We must, Jesus says, abide in the vine if we want to produce fruit. We cannot do it on our strength, but only by abiding in Him.

Wynter was an abider, someone who held on tight to Jesus with full trust, and she was someone who bore much fruit in her life. Her legacy is rich, and her Kingdom impact continues to reverberate around the world.

She did make a difference.

About five months into my season of grieving, my cell phone rang, and when I glanced at who was calling, I was pleasantly surprised. My phone read "Kirk Franklin."

Kirk Franklin is a Grammy-winning songwriter, producer, and gospel music artist, and I had come to know him through Anthony Evans and through my work with Dr. Tony Evans, who was a mentor for Kirk. He was, and is, a larger-than-life figure—one of the few to cross over successfully from the gospel music world to the secular music world and back again. We weren't best friends, but I knew him pretty well from various conversations over the years. He was a thoughtful person and very complimentary to the way that Wynter and I were raising our girls. And he even encouraged our daughter Alena with her singing, once inviting her to sing with him at a family gathering.

I picked up the call.

"Light skin, what's going on?" he said, using the nickname he had given me when we first met due to my lighter skin tone. Over the years it had stuck. Sometimes I wondered if he had ever actually known my name because he always used the nickname!

We made small talk for a bit, then he let me know how much my family and I had been on his mind. How watching us walk through Wynter's death had impressed him with our strength as a family. And how her funeral and the events surrounding it had deeply touched his heart.

Then there was a pause.

What came next was totally unexpected. He said that as a result of all the questions that her passing had raised in his heart, and how it renewed his own longing for heaven, he had written a song. "I was hoping," he said, "that you'd be okay with me naming the song after Wynter. I'd like to call it 'Wynter's Promise.'"

I literally couldn't speak to answer him, overcome by emotions and not knowing what to say. Eventually, I pulled myself together and told him, "Yes, of course." To be able to honor her in this way just filled me with joy and excitement.

Then he dropped another bomb.

"Also, I was wondering if you would be okay with me asking Alena to sing on the recording of the song?"

"Say again?" was all I could manage to say with my now cracking voice.

He explained that there was a vulnerable part in the song where he'd like her honest pain to cry. But he was careful to say that he was okay if she didn't want to do it. I said that I would ask, but I already knew the answer.

Six months to the day after Wynter's passing, the girls and I were sitting in Kirk's studio in Fort Worth, reading the lyrics to the song for the first time and hearing the melody that accompanied them. The song was an inspiring anthem of faith for anyone looking for the hope of heaven. And the song would eventually make its way onto Kirk's newest album, *Long Live Love*, which would win a Grammy for the Gospel Album of the Year. It was called "Wynter's Promise," and it was about how in death we say goodbye to all the shame and pain we have experienced in our lives when we meet Jesus face-to-face. Then our fears will be gone and our tears will be "kissed away."

At the end of the song (you can listen to it on YouTube or your streaming service), Alena ad-libbed a coda where all her raw emotions came surging through; all her heartache about losing her mommy came tumbling out, along with a spoken commitment to carrying on Wynter's legacy. I imagine these were the most difficult words she would ever utter.

She ended her ad-lib with words of hope, confident that her beloved mother was smiling down on her from heaven and looking forward to the day she'll see her again. This was followed by one of Kirk's beautiful melodic piano decrescendos.

I had little understanding of the difficulty that this task would carry for Alena. Had I known, I might have not let her enter into it. But the words that she shared, and the honest pain with which she conveyed them were, I believe, some of the most healing words she would ever speak, and they allowed her to be more vulnerable than she had been up to that moment in time.

It would be several months before we could listen to the finished song. It still carries a weightiness for our family—somber, but ultimately hopeful. Whenever I hear it, I think about the promise God gave Wynter that is enshrined upon that bright pink 3 x 5 index card: "You did not choose me, but I chose you and appointed you that you should go and bear fruit and that your fruit should abide, so that whatever you ask the Father in my name, he may give it to you" (John 15:16).

One translation says that "your fruit should last." Another that "your fruit should remain." Our family has seen the truth of this scripture come to life again and again. Wynter's life on earth had ended, but we believe, by faith, that she is experiencing Jesus and "abiding" in Him now more than ever. Her life produced fruit, and that fruit is lasting. It will endure as long as forever, quite literally from generation to generation.

I can't tell you the number of times I have heard people say, "I didn't know who your wife was, but then I saw her name on Kirk's album, and I heard your daughter's voice. And I had to figure out who she was." What's beautiful in these moments is I get a front-row seat to seeing the continuing impact of her life. I get to bear witness to the beauty I had found in her and share it with others. And I get to honor a woman who gave her life for the cause of the Kingdom of God.

Hopefully, this book, this song, and all these memories add another exclamation point to honoring my wife, my inspiration, my example of abiding in Christ, and my very best friend, Wynter Danielle Pitts.

NOTES

Chapter 4–Final Hours

1. C.S. Lewis, *Till We Have Faces* (New York: Harcourt, 1956), 50.

Chapter 8–Exit Strategy

2. Taken from *What Happens After You Die* by Randy Frazee. Copyright © 2017 by Randy Frazee. Used by permission of Thomas Nelson www.thomasnelson.com.

Chapter 16–Saying Goodbye and Moving On

3. Steven Furtick, "Moving On," used by permission of Syntax Creative, a division of Quality Junk, Inc.

Chapter 18–Be Still

4. Curt Thompson, *The Anatomy of the Soul* (Wheaton, IL: Tyndale, 2010), 118.

Chapter 19–Finishing Well

5. Priscilla Shirer, *Awaken: 90 Days with the God Who Speaks* (Nashville: B & H Books, 2017), 35-36. Used by permission.

Chapter 34–Tents

6. Rebekah Lyons, *You Are Free* (Grand Rapids, MI: Zondervan, 2017).

Acknowledgments

To *Sean Evans*, for entrusting your sister to me.

To *Viola Carter*, for loving me unconditionally and always encouraging me.

To *Miriam and Garry Pitts*, for investing your lives into me and for preparing me for the most difficult day and season of my life.

To the *Pitts family*, for seeing me and loving me unconditionally.

To the *Evans family*, for adopting me from day one and supporting me on this journey.

To *Church of the City*, for adopting me.

To the *For Girls Like You team*, for your commitment to Wynter's legacy and our family's ministry.

To *Harvest House Publishers*, for believing in Wynter, helping her fulfill her life's mission, and for partnering with me to share my story.

To *Alena, Kaitlyn, Camryn, and Olivia*, for trusting me, forgiving me on my worst days, and encouraging me always.

To *Carmen Pitts*, for sacrificing your very life to restore mine.

To *everyone on my journey* who has stepped in as God's angels of light on the darkest of days, thank you.

The angel of the LORD encamps around those
who fear him, and he delivers them.

PSALM 34:7

About the Author

—⟨⟩—

Jonathan Pitts is an author, speaker, and executive pastor at Church of the City in Franklin, Tennessee. Prior to pastoring, Jonathan was executive director at The Urban Alternative, the national ministry of Dr. Tony Evans in Dallas, Texas. Jonathan lives in Franklin, Tennessee, with his four daughters.

For a Marriage That Brims Over

Maybe you entered marriage with some pretty high expectations—most couples do. Jonathan and Wynter Pitts did. Until the reality of married life spilled into their expectations.

Jonathan and Wynter invite you on a journey to explore a different approach to your happily-ever-after marriage. Join them for an honest look at the lessons learned as they navigated the ups and downs of early marriage while raising four daughters.

Here you will...

- be encouraged to remove the pressure of a keeping-up-with-the-Joneses marriage
- learn to let go of assumptions and embrace your role as servant-leader to your spouse
- experience how God can pour His purpose, passion, and fullness into your relationship

Emptied is a way of life. It's not about trying harder; it's about thinking differently. Only when you are emptied of your own self-focused motivations can God pour new life into you for the abundant marriage and satisfying relationship you long for. Are you ready to approach your marriage poured out, ready to be filled up?

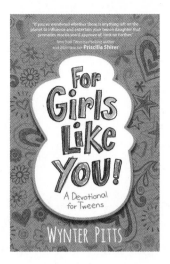

Tween girls have access to an unbelievable amount of media and information with just a simple click of the remote or mouse. Every outlet they turn to attempts to subtly influence their worldview…and what they believe about themselves directly affects how they live.

Wynter Pitts, founder of *For Girls Like You* magazine, gives girls a new devotional showing them a correct definition of themselves, opening their eyes to God's truth and the difference it makes in their lives. Each daily devotion includes a prayer to help girls apply the lesson.

> *"If you've wondered whether there is anything left*
> *on the planet to entertain your young beauties that*
> *promotes morals you'd approve of, look no further."*

AUTHOR AND SPEAKER PRISCILLA SHIRER

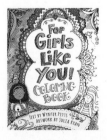

Also available, the *For Girls Like You! Coloring Book.*

To learn more about Harvest House books and
to read sample chapters, visit our website:

www.harvesthousepublishers.com

HARVEST HOUSE PUBLISHERS
EUGENE, OREGON